P9-CMF-364

A PLEA FOR

THE QUEEN'S ENGLISH

" Pædaguli abite pestes,
  Istinc ferte pedem invenusti inepti,
  Invisi pueris bonis malisque,
  Abite in miseram crucem execrati
  Sæcli perniciesque litterarum."

NICCOLÓ, CONTE D' ARCO.
(See Preface).

A PLEA FOR

THE QUEEN'S ENGLISH

Stray Notes on Speaking and Spelling

By HENRY ALFORD, D.D.

DEAN OF CANTERBURY

TENTH THOUSAND

Anchora Spei

ALEXANDER STRAHAN, PUBLISHER

LONDON AND NEW YORK

1866

ALEXANDER STRAHAN, PUBLISHER

LONDON . . . . 148, *Strand*
NEW YORK . . . . . 139, *Grand Street*

INDEX.

PREFACE

TO THE SECOND EDITION.

—•—

THE fact, that an edition consisting of an unusually large number of copies of this little work has been exhausted in a few months, shews that the Public are not indifferent to the interest of the subject. The course of the controversy which it has excited has at all events shewn one thing: that its publication was not un-needed. And though, in the course of this controversy, I have received some hard hits, I have no reason to complain, seeing that it has continually furnished me, as it has gone on, with fresh material for new remarks, and ampler justification for those which I had already made.

A charge has been brought against me, to which I feel bound to reply. One of my censors has alleged that the concluding sentence in paragraph 89 has been altered, so as to convey a sense offensive to him, since its delivery in his hearing at Canterbury.

This allegation is incorrect. That sentence now stands *verbatim* as he heard it delivered here : and let me add, bears no such offensive sense as he supposes.

A mistake occurred in the title-page of the first edition, owing to my absence from England. The title ought to have stood, as will be seen by the first paragraph in that edition, "A Plea for the Queen's English," and now that title has been restored.

I mention this here, because that accidental circumstance has been supposed by one of my censors to conceal I know not what deep purpose, and has been dignified with the name of "the tactics of my opponent."

The motto at the back of the title-page has been borrowed from a little work by Signor Pagliardini, entitled "Essays on the Analogy of Languages." It expresses, in a jocular form, what every one who values our native tongue in its purity must feel : that most of the grammars, and rules, and applications of rules, now so commonly made for our language, are in reality not contributions towards its purity, but main instruments of its deterioration. These rules are often laid down by persons ignorant of the analogy of

languages, of the laws of thought, and of the
practice of those writers whose works are the
great fountain-heads of our English usage. *Diffi-
cile est . . . non scribere*, when we see men whose
knowledge does not extend to the most ordinary
facts of derivation, and requirements of speech,
exalted into authorities whereby to judge of the
correctness of Shakspeare, and Milton, and the
English version of the Bible. We may not
indeed say, *Malim cum Platone errare:* but we
may say confidently, that the old writer had in
his mind some reason for his mode of expression,
which was far above the grasp of his modern
critic.

I am happy to have been, in the course of my
writing these "stray notes," made acquainted
with some modern English Grammars which
form exceptions to the description just given:
Grammars based upon essential facts and principles which are utterly unknown to the "*pœda-
goguli*" of Count d'Arco's epigram.

I may mention among these, Dr. Latham's
sensible English Grammar, and "An English
Grammar specially intended for Classical Schools
and Private Students," by Edward Higginson:
Longmans, 1864.

It now only remains for me to express my
thanks to my many Correspondents, for their

valuable contributions, inquiries, hints, and cor-
rections: to my Censors, both gentle and ungentle,
for their teaching by example and by precept:
and to the Public in general, for the kind interest
which they have shown in these stray notes on
speaking and spelling.

CANTERBURY,
October 28, 1864.

A PLEA FOR

THE QUEEN'S ENGLISH.

1. I have called these "stray notes" "A Introductory. PLEA FOR THE QUEEN'S ENGLISH."

2. I must begin by explaining what I mean by the term. It is one rather familiar and conventional, than strictly accurate. The Queen (God bless her !) is of course no more the proprietor of the English language than any one of us. Nor does she, nor do the Lords and Commons in Parliament assembled, possess one particle of right to make or unmake a word in the language. But we use the phrase, the Queen's English, in another sense ; one not without example in some similar phrases. We speak of the *Queen's Highway*, not meaning that Her Majesty is *possessed* of that portion of road, but that it is a high road of the land, as distinguished from by-roads and private roads : open to all of

common right, and the general property of our country. And so it is with the *Queen's English.* It is, so to speak, this land's great highway of thought and speech; and seeing that the Sovereign in this realm is the person round whom all our common interests gather, the source of our civil duties and centre of our civil rights, the *Queen's English* is not an unmeaning phrase, but one which may serve to teach us some profitable lessons with regard to our language, and its use and abuse.

3. I called our common English tongue the highway of thought and speech; and it may not be amiss to carry on this similitude further. The Queen's highway, now so broad and smooth, was once a mere track over an unenclosed country. It was levelled, hardened, widened, by very slow degrees. Of all this trouble, the passer-by sees no trace now. He bowls along it with ease in a vehicle, which a few centuries ago would have been broken to pieces in a deep rut, or would have come to grief in a bottomless swamp. There were no Croydon baskets, in the day when Henry II. and his train came to do penance from Southampton up that narrow, hollow, rough pilgrims' road, leading over Harbledown Hill to Canterbury.

4. Now just so is it with our English language—our Queen's English. There was a day when it was as rough as the primitive inhabitants. Centuries have laboured at levelling, hardening, widening it. For language wants all these processes, as well as roads do. In order to become a good highway for thought and speech, it must not have great prominent awkward points, over which the mind and the tongue may stumble ; its words must not be too weak to carry the weight of our thoughts, nor its limiting rules too narrow to admit of their extension. And it is by processes of this kind in the course of centuries, that our English tongue has been ever adapted more and more to our continually increasing wants. It has never been found too rough, too unsubstantial, too limited, for the requirements of English thought. It has become for us, in our days, a level, firm, broad highway, over which all thought and all speech can travel smoothly and safely. Along it the lawyer and the parliamentary agent propel their heavy waggons, clogged with a thousand pieces of cumbrous antiquated machinery,—and no wonder, when they charge freightage, not by the weight of the load, combined with the distance, but by the number of impediments

which they can manage to offer to the progress of their vehicle. Along it the poet and novelist drive their airy tandems, dependent for their success on the dust which they raise, and through which their varnished equipages glitter. On the same road divines, licensed and unlicensed, ply once a week or more, with omnibus or carrier's cart, promising to carry their passengers into another land than that over which the road itself extends, just as the coaches out of London used to astonish our boyish eyes by the "*Havre de Grace*" and "*Paris*" inscribed on them. And along this same Queen's highway plods ever the great busy crowd of foot-passengers—the talkers of the market, of society, of the family. Words, words, words; good and bad, loud and soft, long and short; millions in the hour, innumerable in the day, unimaginable in the year: what then in the life? what in the history of a nation? what in that of the world? And not one of these is ever forgotten. There is a book where they are all set down. What a history, it has been well said, is this earth's atmosphere, seeing that all words spoken, from Adam's first till now, are still vibrating on its sensitive and unresting medium.

5. But it is not so much of the great high-

way itself of Queen's English that I would now speak, as of some of the laws and usages of the road; the by-rules, so to speak, which hang up framed at the various stations, that all may read them.

6. I have called the contents of these pages "Stray notes on speaking and spelling." The things of which I have to treat are for the most part insulated and unconnected; so that I fear there will not be even the appearance of connection between the various parts of my volume. And again, it must be confessed that they are not of a very interesting kind. I shall have to speak of such dull things as parts of speech, and numbers, and genders; the obscuration, or the conventional and licensed violation, of rules of grammar, and the pronunciation and spelling of words.

7. It will be necessary perhaps to state that the things of which I am going to speak are not to be looked upon as altogether of a trifling character. One of my critics, of whom I shall have more to say further on, thinks it ludicrous and absurd that a dignitary of the Church of England should meddle with such small matters. But the language of a people is no trifle. The national mind is reflected in the national speech. If the way in which men

The matter in hand no trifle.

express their thoughts is slipshod and mean, it will be very difficult for their thoughts themselves to escape being the same. If it is high-flown and bombastic, a character for national simplicity and truthfulness, we may be sure, cannot be long maintained. That nation must be (and it has ever been so in history) not far from rapid decline, and from being degraded from its former glory. Every important feature in a people's language is reflected in its character and history.

Examples:
American
debase-
ments.

8. Look, to take one familiar example, at the process of deterioration which our Queen's English has undergone at the hands of the Americans. Look at those phrases which so amuse us in their speech and books; at their reckless exaggeration, and contempt for congruity ; and then compare the character and history of the nation—its blunted sense of moral obligation and duty to man ; its open disregard of conventional right where aggrandizement is to be obtained; and, I may now say, its reckless and fruitless maintenance of the most cruel and unprincipled war in the history of the world. Such examples as this (and they are as many as the number of the nations and their tongues) may serve to show that language is no trifle.

9. Then, again, carefulness about minute Chatterton's
imposture. accuracies of inflexion and grammar may appear to some very contemptible. But it would be just as easy to give examples in refutation of this idea. Two strike me, of widely different kinds. Some years ago a set of poems was published at Bristol, purporting to have been written in very early times by a poet named Rowley. Literary controversy ran high about them; many persons believed in their genuineness; some do even now. But the imposture, which was not easy to detect at the time, has been now completely unmasked by the aid of a little word of three letters. The writer uses "*its*" as the possessive case of the pronoun "it" of the neuter gender. Now this possessive "*its*" was never used in the early periods of our language; nor, indeed, as late down as Elizabeth. It never occurs in the English version of the Bible, made in its present authorized form in the reign of James I. :* "*his*" or "*her*" being

---

* We have it in one place in our present copies, viz., Levit. xxv. 5 : "That which groweth of *its* own accord." But this has been an alteration by the printers : King James's authorized copies have "of it own accord :" just as Shakspeare wrote (see notice of the Cambridge Shakspeare in the "Times" of Sept. 29, 1863) "The innocent milk in it most innocent mouth :" and "go to it grandam, child, and it grandam

always used instead. "They came unto the iron gate that leadeth unto the city; which opened to them of *his* own accord" (Acts xii. 10). "Of beaten work made he the candlestick; *his* shaft, and *his* branch, *his* bowls, *his* knops, and *his* flowers, were of the same" (Ex. xxxvii. 17). "The tree of life, which yielded *her* fruit every month" (Rev. xxii. 2). It is said also only to occur three times in Shakspeare, and once in "Paradise Lost." The reason, I suppose, being, that possession, indicated by the possessive case "*its*," seemed to imply a certain life or personality, which things neuter could hardly be thought of as having.

Detection of St. Peter by his speech.

10. The other example is one familiar to you, of a more solemn character. When St. Peter was stoutly denying all knowledge of his suffering Master, they that stood by said to him, "Surely thou art one of them; for thou art a Galilean, and thy speech agreeth thereto." So that the fact of a provincial pronunciation was made use of to bring about the repentance of an erring apostle.

11. This little book will be found to justify

will give it a plum." The usage of "*it*" for "*its*," is still found in the provincial talk of the Midland and Northern counties. (See on this subject Dr. Latham's "History of the English Language," pp. 527-9, 589.)

the description on its title, which represents it as consisting of "Stray notes." These were written down during the intervals of more serious employment, to serve as matter for lectures to the "Church of England Young Men's Literary Association" at Canterbury. Having performed that duty, they were published in the widely circulated periodical entitled "Good Words;" and now, in a considerably altered form, they are presented to the public.

12. As the lectures were given, and the articles were published, considerable controversy sprang up respecting many points which were noticed in them. Correspondence became very abundant, and full of amusement and interest, and the second and third essays assumed something of a controversial character. On collecting them, however, into a volume, I found it desirable to omit very much that referred to matters in dispute; and in this second edition, I have carried this omission further, and struck out or modified most of the notices which pointed at individual antagonists.

13. The few allusions to matters of controversy which have been still retained, are those which seemed necessary, as immediately con-

cerning the subjects under treatment. While
striking out all that was merely vindicative
of myself in refutation of an opponent, I have
been unwilling to part with arguments which,
though contributing to that end also, yet
were chiefly auxiliary to the main objects
which I had in view.

Omitting
the "u" in
words in
"-our." 14. The first remark that I have to make
shall be on the trick now so universal across
the Atlantic, and becoming in some quarters
common among us in England, of leaving
out the "*u*" in the termination "*-our;*"
writing *honor, favor, neighbor, Savior,* &c.
Now the objection to this is, not that it
makes very ugly words, totally unlike anything in the English language before (for we
do thus spell some of the words thus derived,
for example, *author, governor, emperor,* &c.),
but that it is part of a movement to reduce
our spelling to uniform rule as opposed to
usage, and to help forward the obliteration
of all trace of the derivation and history of
words. It is true that *honor* and *favor* are
derived *originally* from Latin words spelt
exactly the same ; but it is also true that
we did not get them direct from the Latin,
but through the French forms, which ended
in "*-eur.*" Sometimes words come through

as many as three steps before they reach
us—

> "'Twas Greek at first; that Greek was Latin made:
> That Latin, French; that French to English straid."

15. The late Archdeacon Hare, in an article
on English Orthography in the "Philological
Museum," some years ago, expressed a hope
that "such abominations as *honor* and *favor*
would henceforth be confined to the cards of
the great vulgar." There we still see them,
and in books printed in America; and while
we are quite contented to leave our fashionable friends in such company, I hope we may
none of us be tempted to join **it**.*

16. We have spoken of these words in "neighbour."
"*our*" as mostly having come to us from the
Latin in "*or*," through the French in "*eur*."
It has been observed, that this is not the case
with some words involved in the "or" and

---

* Much has been made of the fact of some of these
transatlantic spellings being found in the last edition of
my own poems. But, as will be seen on referring to the
advertisement to that edition, the main part of the
printer's work was done in America, and my own
spelling was altered there. The occurrence of "favored"
and "odors" in one of the last poems in the volume, is
owing to that, with some other pieces, having formed
part of an imperfect sheet in the American edition, and
having been, in making up the additional sheets in the
English volume, reprinted without correction.

"our" question. One of these is "*neighbour.*„
This has come from the German "*nachbar ;*"*
and it is therefore urged, that an exception
should be made in its case to the ending with
our, and it should be written "*neighbor.*" I
am afraid the answer must be, that English
custom has ruled the practice another way,
and has decided the matter for us. We do
not follow rule in spelling the other words,
but custom. We write *senator, orator, governor*, in spite of the French *senateur, orateur,
gouverneur*. If we once begin reforming our
spelling on rule, we ought to be consistent,
and to carry our principles throughout. It is
only the maintenance of our national custom
and usage for which a reasonable man can
plead. We have no Academy to settle such
things for us ; and as long as neighbour is
universally spelt in England with a "*u*," I fear
we must be content to conform, even though
it appear to have been first so spelt by those

---

* It appears that the derivation of neighbour from
the German *nachbar* is questioned. I have had a
letter from a Danish correspondent, who charges me
with error in stating this as its derivation, and believes it to come from the Danish or rather Norse, *nabo*,
compounded from the words *nær*, near, and *boe*, to live
or dwell. I observe, moreover, that the dictionaries
derive it from the Anglo-Saxon "nehʒebur : " in which
case the *u* has more right in the word than the *o*.

who forgot its derivation. It is when custom is various, and some rule is needed to decide which variety is right, that I have advocated the application of rules in order to that decision.

17. In the case of another word thus "control." variously spelt, *control,* the rule is plain, and general usage conforms to it. Control never acquired any right to be spelt with a "*u.*" It comes from the French *contrôle, i.e., contrerôle:* and the original meaning is still found in the name *Controller,* when applied to finance : *i.e.,* an officer whose duty it is to keep a counter-roll, or check on the accounts of others. It seems also clear, from this account of the word, that it ought not to be spelt *compt,* as it frequently is, but *cont.*

18. With regard to one word of the class "tenor" and "tonour." under consideration, *tenor,* it has been alleged that it bears different senses, according as we spell it with or without *u* in the last syllable : *tenour* signifying the character, or complexion, or drift of a course of action or speaking ; and *tenor* signifying the part in music. But I can find no such distinction observed, either by writers, or by the compilers of our dictionaries. Some dictionaries give teno*r* for both, some teno*ur ;* and with regard to usage, the

distinction attempted to be set up is certainly
not observed. Sir Philip Sidney, Shakspeare, Dryden, Pope, Waterland, Locke, all
use *tenor* in the sense of the *constant mode*, or
manner of continuity, as may be seen in the
dictionaries. The distinction is observed in
French, but never appears to have been made
a point of in English : and the word thus remains in the same predicament as the rest of
those in this class—subject to be varied this
way or that, according to prevailing usage.

Phonetic spelling.

19. When I published my first paper in
"Good Words," I wrote to this effect :—"The
omission of the '*u*' is an approach to that
wretched attempt to destroy all the historic
interest of our language, which is known by
the name of *phonetic* spelling ; concerning
which we became rather alarmed some years
ago, when we used to see on our reading-room
tables a journal published by the advocates of
this change, called the 'Phonetic News,' but
from its way of spelling looking like *Frantic
Nuts*. The whole thing has now, I believe,
disappeared, and gone into the limbo of abor-
tive schemes ; the knacker's yard of used-up
hobbies." This sentence gave great offence
to the supporters of the so-called spelling-
reform. I had imagined that their endeavour

to substitute irrational for rational spelling had entirely failed, and died away; and I expressed myself accordingly. It appears that it is still going on, and that the "Phonetic Journal," its organ, has attained a circulation of 1,000 : no very large figure certainly, considering the number of years during which the movement has existed. I have stated the fact, as I was requested to do : but I cannot change my opinion either as to the character or as to the prospects of the movement. Its character may be in some measure illustrated by the view which its promoters seem to take of the facts of etymology. Enclosed in a letter of remonstrance to me was a copy of a reprint by them of Dean Swift's burlesque, in which he facetiously proves that the Greek and Latin tongues were derived from the English, making out that *Andromache* was *Andrew Mackay*, and the like. Here is a rich specimen. " Alexander the Great was very fond of eggs roasted in hot ashes. As soon as his cooks heard he was come to dinner or supper, they called aloud to their under-officers, '*All eggs under the grate*,' which, repeated every day at noon and evening, made strangers think it was that prince's real name, and they therefore gave him no other : and posterity has been ever since under the same delusion."

20. Now it is one thing to write or to enjoy a joke, and another to use it with a view to an ulterior purpose. It is natural that those who are obliterating the traces of the historical formation of the language, should endeavour to cast ridicule on etymologists ; but it is not easy to say why they should have republished Swift's squib, if, as they profess, their system tends to *preserve* the history of the language, and not to efface it.

21. And as to the future, I cannot bring myself to believe that the system will ever prevail generally among English writers. It is a good thing to devise every means by which a short-hand writer,—whose object is to note down with all speed what he hears,—may be enabled to abridge his work. Let it by all means set at nought conventional spelling, and use what symbols he finds most convenient for the sounds expressed by combined letters. But *our* object is not expeditious writing only, nor is it easy spelling, nor uniformity in expressing the same sounds. We use, in writing, an instrument which has been adapted to our use by nearly sixty centuries ; which bears on it the marks of many

a conflict of thought and belief; whose very uncertainties and anomalies are records of our intercourse with other nations, and of the agglomeration of our mingled English people. You may gain, with no great trouble, uniformity of spelling, and of pronunciation according to spelling; but you will do it at the sacrifice of far more than the gain is worth. A smooth front of stucco may be a comely thing for those that like it; but very few sensible men will like it, if they know that, in laying it on, we are proposing to obliterate the roughnesses, and mixture of styles, and traces of architectural **transition**, from the venerable front of an ancient cathedral. I have fulfilled my promise to my phonetic correspondent, and announced that my former statement was not correct. I can only say I am sorry for it, and express a hope that it may not be long before the result then anticipated is fully accomplished.

22. In a letter received from another phonetic correspondent, I learn that there is division in the camp. The gentleman who is by his own followers characterized as the apostle of the movement, is by the other party regarded as the principal hindrance to its progress. So that the end may not be far

off after all. I also learn from this later correspondent, that it is only the *short-hand department* of the phonetic movement which can at all be described as being in a flourishing state; and to that I wish all prosperity, provided always that it rises on the ruins of the other.

"-ent" and "-ant." 23. Here is another instance, in which our acknowledged English custom in spelling seems to defy all rule. How does it stand with the words ending in *-ent* and *-ant,* derived from the participles of Latin verbs? Some of these follow rule, others depart from it. The first conjugation of Latin verbs, forming its participle in *-ans,* genitive *-antis,* gives rise to a set of derivatives in our language which keep constant to the termination *-ant.* We have *abundant, reluctant, exuberant, remonstrant, recusant, recalcitrant,* and the rest. But in the case of the second, third, and fourth Latin conjugations, forming their participles in *-ens,* genitive *-entis,* we have not been able to keep the derivatives steady to the original type. In the greater number of cases, they follow it: in some, usage varies; in a few, they have rejected the primitive form, and have adopted the *-ent.* We always write *different* and *difference;* indeed the deri-

vative *differential* seems to fix these forms on
us, as *transcendental* fixes *transcendent*. *De-pendent* and *dependant* seem to be written in-differently. But *defendant* and *attendant* are
universal. In some cases, the rules of pronun-ciation have kept the *-ent* unvaried. Take for
instance the derivatives from Latin verbs end-ing in *-esco*,—*crescent, quiescent, acquiescence,
arborescent* : and such words as *detergent, emer-gency.* In all these, the substitution of *a* for
e would change the soft sound of the pre-ceding consonant into a hard one : we should
be obliged to say *creschant, deterghant,* &c.

23*a*. The question, *in-* or *en-*, in words
beginning with the preposition variously
thus represented in Latin and French, seems
utterly to defy any answer according to rule.
" Engrave," " enrich," " engross," " enrol," are
universal ; but so are "infant," "intent," "in-flame :" while we have both " enquire" and
" inquire," both " enclose" and " inclose,'
both " endorse" and " indorse," used indif-ferently. We have also " insurance" and
" assurance" indifferently used ; and the
liberty of choice in this case is owing to the
fact that we may use both verbs, to *assure*
and to *insure,* of that kind of making safe,
which the substantive represents.

24. There seems to be considerable doubt in the public mind how to spell the two words *ecstasy* and *apostasy*. The former of these especially is a puzzle to our compositors and journalists. Is it to be *extasy, extacy, ecstacy,* or *ecstasy ?* The question is at once decided for us by the Greek root of the word. This is *ecstasis* (ἔκστασις), a standing, or position, out of, or beside, one's-self. The same is the case with apostasy. The root of this is *apostasis* (ἀπόστασις), a standing off or away from a man's former position. Consequently, *ecstasy* (or, if we prefer it, *extasy*) and apostasy, are right, not those forms which end in *-cy*.

25. *Lay* and *lie* seem not yet to be settled. Few things are more absurd than the confusion of these two words. To "*lay*" is a verb active transitive : a hen *lays* eggs. To "*lie*" is a verb neuter ; a sluggard *lies* in bed. Whenever the verb *lay* occurs, something must be supplied after it ; the proper rejoinder to "Sir, there it lays," would be "*lays what ?*" The reason of the confusion has been, that the past tense of the neuter verb "*lie*" is "*lay*," looking very like part of the active verb :—"I lay in bed this morning." But this, again, is perverted into *laid*,

which belongs to the other verb. I have observed that Eton men, for some reason or other, are especially liable to confuse these two verbs.

26. There seems to be some doubt occasionally felt about the apostrophe which marks the genitive case singular. One not uncommonly sees outside an inn, that "*fly's*" and "*gig's*" are to be let. In a country town blessed with more than one railway, I have seen an omnibus with "RAILWAY STATION'S" painted in emblazonry on its side.

The apostrophe of the genitive singular.

27. It is curious, that at one time this used to be, among literary men, the usual way of writing the plurals of certain nouns. In the "Spectator," as a correspondent reminds me, Addison writes "*Purcell's opera's*" with an apostrophe before the "*s*". And we find "*the making of grotto's*" mentioned as a favourite employment of ladies in that day.

28. Occasionally this apostrophe before the "*s*" in plurals is adopted to avoid an awkward incongruous appearance : as in another instance from the "Spectator" given by my correspondent, where Addison speaks of the way in which some people use "their *who's* and their whiches." Certainly "*whos*" would be an awkward-looking word, and so would

"*whoes*." It would seem as if we were compelled to admit the intruder in these cases : for without him, how should we ever be able to express in writing that people drop their *h's*, or omit to dot their *i's* and cross their *t's*? But if we do, we must carefully bar the gate again, and refuse to tolerate his presence in any plurals where he is not absolutely required.

29. I have observed, on the part of our advertising post-horse-keepers, a strange reluctance to give the proper plural of *fly*, used to denote a vehicle. Where we do not see *fly's*, we commonly find "*flys*" instead, and very rarely indeed "*flies*," the obvious and only legitimate plural : the reason apparently being, that there is a fear of a ludicrous meaning being suggested by the word. But if we do not think of the insect when we see "*fly*" in the singular, why should the plural form necessarily raise the thought in our minds ?

29*a*. A correspondent raises the question, whether the name of the carriage be not really derived from the verb, seeing that certain night-coaches were once called "*fly-by-night*"? And if so, why, he asks, should it be required to follow the rule of the sub-

stantive? But we may answer, was not that
substantive itself also, in its time, derived
from the verb? It is not merely the analogy
of this particular substantive, but that of the
language, to which we would bind the new
noun.

30. A dispute was referred to me by the
compositors of a certain journal, as to whether
we ought to write *Messrs. Jacksons works* with
the apostrophe before the final "*s*" in *Jacksons*, or after it : in other words—for it comes
to the same—whether, in speaking of the
firm, we ought to say Messrs. *Jackson*, or
Messrs. *Jacksons*. It seems to me that, by
using the plural appellative *Messieurs*, we
have already adopted the former of these.
Each member of the firm is Mr. Jackson : we
may regard the whole firm, if we will, as
made up of *Mr.-Jacksons*. But in speaking
of the firm as a whole, we use the other form,
and say the *Messrs. Jackson*. It is plain that
we have no right to mix both forms together,
and to say the *Messrs. Jacksons*, with both
names in the plural. So that, the practice of
the commercial world having bound us to
speak of the Messrs. Jackson,—when we speak
of *Messrs. Jacksons works*, the apostrophe or
sign of the genitive case ought to come before

the final *s* (Messrs. Jackson's works), and not after it (Messrs. Jacksons' works). The example by which the other side in the dispute defended their view, was ingeniously chosen, but did not apply. They urged that in writing "*nine months imprisonment*," the apostrophe is put, not before, but after, the final *s* in months. Certainly: because we cannot say, and never do say, *nine month* : whereas we can and do always say, *Messrs. Jackson.*

What is the apostrophe ?

31. We are led on by our last paragraph to say something about this same apostrophe itself.* First, what is it ? what does it mean ? When I speak of "*the Senator*" in one sentence, and of "*the Senator's son*" in another, what has happened to the word *Senator* in becoming *Senator's,* with the apostrophe ? The question was at one time answered by saying that "*the Senator's son*" was an abbreviation of "*the Senator, his son.*" And we may remember that the prayer for all conditions of men in our Common Prayer book ends with the words "*for Jesus Christ his sake.*" But more attention showed that this was an erroneous view of the matter. It failed to account for all feminine genitives: "*your wife's father*" cannot be "*your wife his father;*" and for all

* See note A, end of the volume.

plural genitives: the children's bread cannot be "*the children his bread.*" More attention shewed that the *s* preceded by the apostrophe is an abbreviation of the added syllable "*-is,*" marking the possessive or genitive case. Thus "*the Senator's son*" in English answers to *Senatoris filius* in Latin.

32. But if *the Senator's son*, with an apostrophe between the *r* and *s*, signifies *the son of the Senator*, how am I to express in a similar form *the sons of the Senators?* in other words, what becomes of the apostrophe when we want to make a possessive case in the plural? We have no inflexion, as in *Senatorum filii*, by which it can be expressed. Can we use the final *-is* to mark the possessive in the plural as we do in the singular? It would seem to a Latin scholar absurd so to do; yet we do it. We have already cited *the children's bread.* But most of our plural nouns already end in *s*; and to them we do not superadd another *s* with the apostrophe, but indicate its omission by simply putting the apostrophe after the plural noun. We say "*the senators' sons:*" "*the senators' sons' wives:*" "*the senators' sons' wives' jewels.*" I mention this, not to inform any one of so well known a practice, but because it gives rise to a few cases in which there is some

difficulty. The reason of the usage may be, that we may avoid the occurrence of the two sibilant letters together. This seems likely, because we extend it to other words ending in *s*, or in a sound like *s*, though they may not be plural. Thus we say, "for thy goodness' sake," meaning, for the sake of thy goodness : in which case the word "goodness" ought plainly to be written with the apostrophe after it. Thus, too, we should say "for patience' sake," meaning, for the sake of patience ; and again, we ought to put the apostrophe after "patience."

33. But we are not consistent in this. If we were speaking of a *person named* Patience, we should say, "*Patience's* father is here": and we form the possessive cases of James, and Thomas, and Charles, not by the mere apostrophe, but by the apostrophe with the *s*. "Thomas is Charles's son : James is Thomas's son ; therefore Charles is James's grandfather." Again, we say and write Bass's Ale, not Bass' Ale : Chambers's Journal, not Chambers' Journal.

Plurals of compound names.

34. Very nearly related to the last question is the following. Which of these two is right, —the *Misses Brown,* or the *Miss Browns ?* For the former it may be said, that *Brown* is

the name of the whole species, and that the young ladies, being individuals of that species, are *Misses;* for the latter, that each of the young ladies being *Miss-Brown,* the whole taken together, or any two or more, are *Miss-Browns.* So that either way is justifiable. Usage is all but universal in favour of the latter in conversation. We may say we met *the Miss Browns,* not *the Misses Brown.* But we can hardly justify this our colloquial practice, if we bring in *Mrs. Brown,* and say we met *Mrs. and the Miss Browns.* For, by enumerating thus first the individual, and then the species, we bind ourselves to the *former* way of spelling. The sentence, as I have last given it, is inaccurate ; because it really says that we met *Mrs., and the Miss, Browns ;* i.e., one *Mrs.* and *one celebrated Miss,* rejoicing in the name of, not *Brown,* but *Browns.* If we had wished to keep to the ordinary colloquial usage in this case also, we ought to have said that we met *Mrs. Brown and the Miss Browns.*

35. A correspondent writes :—" We sometimes hear people speak of *calves'-head.* I have seen it written so on bills of fare, meaning a dish made of the *head of a calf.* The same people would in all probability say 'two

calves' heads,' meaning two dishes, each of
which is called '*calf's-head.*' I should prefer
to say 'two *calf's-heads.*' This is not mentioned in any work on English Grammar."

35*a.* A correspondent asks, whether of these
two is right, "*spoonfuls*" or "*spoonsfull.*"
The answer seems very obvious. If spoonful
is to be regarded as one word, as I suppose it
is, then spoonfuls is its plural. "The earth
brought forth by handfuls" (Gen. xli. 47).
But if we keep the compounding syllables
separate, *a spoon full,* then we ought of course
to say two spoons full, and so on.

"attor-
neys" and
"moneys." 36. There seems to be a liability to error
in the formation of some plurals themselves.
The words "*attorney*" and "*money*" are often
made into "*attornies*" and "*monies*" in the
plural. This is of course wrong : we might
as well turn the singular "*key*" into a plural
"*kies.*" I am not aware that any one ever
wrote "*monkies*" or "*donkies*" for "*monkeys*"
or "*donkeys.*" And this is not a case of rule
against usage : for all our better and more
careful writers use the right plurals, viz.,
"*attorneys,*" and "*moneys.*"

means." 37. A question arises as to the proper construction of certain nouns bearing the plural
form. The first which I shall notice is "*means.*"

" Those pieces of hypocrisy were, with him,
means to an end." " That piece of hypocrisy
was with him, a"—what ?—a *mean* to an end ?
No,—this is not English, though it may be correct in grammatical construction. " That piece
of hypocrisy was, with him, a *means* to an end."
This is how we speak. And we say, " the
best *means* of accomplishing your end *is*," if
we are going to speak of one mode of action
only ; not " the best *mean* is," nor " the best
means are," unless we mean to enumerate
more than one.

38. Very similar is our way of dealing with " news."
" *news*." If we are about to mention one fact
only, we say the latest news " *is*," not " *are*."
In this case indeed the use of the plural verb
at all is unusual, even if several things are to
be mentioned. If we pick one out of several,
we sometimes say, " The latest *piece of
news* is." " Here lies the remains of," has
been justified, on the ground that " *remains*"
is equivalent to " remainder," there being no
such singular noun as " *a remain*." But the
defence is unquestionably wrong. The word
" *remains*" is, and is intended to be, plural, in
signification, as well as in form. The human
body is broken up by death, and is no longer
regarded as a whole, but as a heap of decom-

posing parts. And the same idea is present
in speaking of any thing which has passed
into decay or dismemberment : we speak commonly of *the ruins* of a church or castle,
though in this case we may say that it has
become " *a ruin :*" we have "les restes,"
" trümmer," "rudera," " ἐρείπια," all plurals.

"mewses."   39. There is another word which I was not
aware had become one of this class, till I
perceived on the London walls an undoubted
proof that it had. I mean " *mews.*" I should
have been inclined to say, " South Portman
Mews are on the left as you go up Orchard
Street." But clearly this is not the way
of speaking which is most intelligible to the
coachmen and grooms of London. For at the
entrance of every one of the Marylebone mews
(I am using my own plural), I see a notice
posted for the regulation of the " *mewses*" of
the metropolis.* Besides the incongruity of
its poetic associations, this word " *mewses*" is
a very queer monster. Fancy ordering " *two
Daily Newses,*" by way of two copies of the

---

* In my article printed in "Good Words" for Novem-
ber, 1863, I had supposed this form of the notice to be
current throughout London, and had ascribed it to Sir
Richard Mayne. I received the following letter from
Dr. Thomson, the medical officer of health for Maryle-

"Daily News." Still, we must allow the Marylebone parish authorities this much indulgence, as to confess that their word is not altogether without precedent. With regard to *summons*, which appears to be another of u,s,m-mons." these plural words become singular, and in the usage of which we have long ago become accustomed to read that "*summonses* were served on all the offenders," a barrister has suggested to me that it is in fact derived

bone, which enables me to correct my former statement :—

"DEPARTMENT OF MEDICAL OFFICER OF HEALTH.
   "*Court House, St. Marylebone, W.*
         "November 5, 1863.

"SIR,—I observe that in your last interesting paper on the English language in 'Good Words,' you ascribe the use of the term Mewses to Sir Richard Mayne. In justice to him, allow me to state that the regulations to which you refer are only attached, so far as I am aware, to the Mews in the parish of St. Marylebone. They were drawn up by myself, and in my original copy of the draught they are styled Mews. In correcting the proofs, however, the legal authorities of the parish substituted the term you object to, in defiance of the Queen's English, but in direct obedience to the inexorable 35 Geo. 3, cap. 73, passed in 1795, where the term Mewses occurs throughout.

         "Very faithfully yours,
            "R. DUNDAS THOMSON, M.D., F.R.S.
               "Medical Officer of Health.
"The Very Reverend the Dean of Canterbury."

from the French "*semonce.*" Probability is
given to this idea, from the fact that the verb
representing the serving of the legal process,
is in English most commonly pronounced, not
to "summon," but to "summon*s*," as it naturally would be, if from the French verb
"*semoncer.*" In Landais' large French dictionary, the meanings are thus given :—

Semonce, subst. fem. (du latin *submonitio*,
fait de *submonere*, avertir secrètement, à demi-
mot), invitation faite dans les formes pour
quelque cérémonie.—Avertissement fait par
quelqu'un qui a autorité.—Reprimande.

Semoncer, v. act., faire une *semonce :* donner
un avertissement.

So that, at all events, the proposed derivation is not far-fetched ; for the signification exactly corresponds. The only "missing
link" is, the historical proof, from the old
French of our courts, that "*semonce*" and
"*semoncer*" were actually used in them,
and from French passed into English. This,
which I am not able to give, some of my
legal correspondents may perhaps supply. I
observe that Todd, in his edition of Johnson,
derives summons from the formal Latin name
of the writ, "*summoneas.*" But this does not
seem so probable.

40. Ought the district over which a bishop has ecclesiastical jurisdiction to be spelt *diocese,* or *diocess?* The latter form is found in a few of our older writers, and is by some persons retained in our own days. The "Times" newspaper seems pertinaciously to adhere to it. I have observed that, in letters inserted and extracts given, the spelling is even altered to this form. But there is really no justification for it. It seems to have come from the Norman-French *diocisse;* but the derivation of the word, as well as the usage of the great majority of English writers, fixes the spelling the other way. The word is derived from the Greek "*dioikēsis,*" with the "*eta*" or long *e* in the last syllable but one ; and ought no more to be spelt diocess, than *cheese* ought to be spelt *chess.*

" diocess " or " diocese."

41. The division of a word, when the former portion has to be written in one line and the latter in another, may seem but a trifling matter ; but it is one worth a few moments' attention. The ordinary rule is, that the break should be so made, as to let the new line begin with a consonant. And notice that this is not the same matter as division of the word into its component parts. This latter process must follow the order of

Division of a word between lines.

D

derivation and inflexion of the word : but in
division between line and line, we are obliged
to transgress this order. For instance, in
dividing the word *attainted* into its component parts, we say that *at-* is the first, *taint-*
the second, and *-ed* the third : *taint* being the
root of the word, and *-ed* the added sign of
the past tense. But in dividing this word
between two lines, we should put *attain-* in
the former line, and *-ted* in the latter. If
any one is disposed to object to this way of
dividing, and to require that we should in all
cases follow the composition and inflexion of
the word, and begin the new line with the *-ed,*
he may at once be shown the impossibility of
doing so, by trying it in the case of any verb
ending with *e* preceded by a mute and a
liquid, as *humble,* or any which turns a final *y*
into *ie,* as *multiply,* in making its past tense.
The word *humbled* is confessedly of two syllables : but if we are to divide on the *rational*
plan, where is the break to occur ? It is true
that, in this particular case, on no plan is the
account to be given quite satisfactory. The
pronunciation of the word in reading, making
the *e* of *ed* mute, may be represented by
" *humbld.*" But this is not expressed by
hum-bled, nor by *humb-led,* nor indeed by any

mode of division that can be devised. The
inference is, that we should, if possible, avoid
dividing such a word at all. But in such
words as *multiplied*, though the rational division according to inflexion fails, the ordinary
rule is easily followed : *-plied*, when the *e* is
mute, becomes the last syllable, and the division is made accordingly.

42. I have observed that Mr. Charles "to" and
"too."
Dickens speaks in one of his works of
"shutting *too*." Now it is true that "*to*"
and "*too*" are originally the same word; in
German, *zu* expresses them both; but it is
also true that usage with us has appropriated
"*too*" for the adverb of addition or excess,
and "*to*" for the preposition; and that in
the expression "shutting *to*," it is the preposition, and not the adverb that is used; that
to which the door is shut being omitted, and
the preposition thus getting the adverbial
sense of *close* or *home*.

43. There seems to be a habit of express- Doubling
the final
ing any less usual sense of a monosyllabic letter.
word by doubling the final letter. Thus I
have sometimes seen "This house to *lett*."
And in one of the numerous mining circulars
which are constantly swelling one's daily
parcel of letters, I observe it stated, that the

"*sett*" is very rich and promising. Thus, likewise, *clear* profit is sometimes described as "*nett*," instead of "*net*."

44. This reminds us of another doubling of a final letter, respecting which there is considerable doubt. Does the verb to *benefit*, in forming its past participle, double its final letter? Is it true, as stated in the first edition of this work, that this doubling only takes place in a syllable on which the accent is laid, and that the purpose of it is to ensure the right pronunciation? At first sight it would seem so. If the participle of quit were spelt *quited*, it would be pronounced as in *requited*, and would lose the sound of its verb: whereas by spelling it *quitted*, that sound is retained. And so of fit, rebel, abhor, and other words of the same kind. When the syllable has no accent on it, the reduplication seems not to be needed, for there can be but one way of pronouncing it; we might as well make the participle of *remember*, *rememberred*, as that of *benefit*, *benefitted*. But the intelligent Irish correspondent, whom I quote at length on paragraph 225, observes justly that this view does not seem borne out in the case of *cavilling*, *travelling*, *grovelling*, and the like words. So that, after all, it seems

as if usage were our only safe guide in the matter.

45. I have several times noticed, and once in a letter censuring some of my own views on the Queen's English, the verb to *lose* spelt *loose*. A more curious instance of the arbitrary character of English usage as to spelling and pronunciation, could hardly be given, than these two words furnish: but usage must be obeyed. In this case it is not consistent with itself in either of the two practices: the syllable "*-oose*" keeps the sound of "*s*" in *loose, noose, goose*, but changes it for that of "*z*" in *choose*: the syllable "*-ose*" keeps the sound of "*s*" in *close, dose*, but changes it for that of "*z*" in *chose, hose, nose, pose, rose*. But when usage besides this requires us to give the "*o*" in *lose* the sound of "*u*" in *luminary*, we feel indeed that reasoning about spelling and pronunciation is almost at an end.

46. San*itary* and san*atory* are but just beginning to be rightly understood. San*itary*, from *sanitas*, Latin for soundness or health, means, appertaining to *health;* san*atory*, from *sano*, to cure, means appertaining to *healing* or *curing*. "The town is in such a bad sanitary condition, that some sanatory mea-

" lose *"* and *"* loose.*"*

" sanitary*"* and *"* sana*-*tory.*"*

sures must be undertaken." I was surprised
to see, in the *Illustrated News* of October 31, 1863, a print and description of
Murree, one of the "*Sanitariums*" for our
troops in India.

" Pharaoh."   47. I have noticed that the title of the
ancient Egyptian kings hardly ever escapes
mis-spelling. That title is Pha*raoh*, not Pha-
roah. Yet a leading article in the *Times*, not
long since, was full of PHAROAH, printed, as
proper names in leading articles are, in conspicuous capitals. Nay, even worse than this :
on my first visit to the South Kensington
Museum, an institution admirably calculated
to teach the people, I found a conspicuous
notice with the same mis-spelling in it. I
gave a memorandum of it to the attendant ;
but whether it has been corrected or not I
cannot say.

Mis-spelling
in news-
papers.   48. It is in newspapers, and especially in
provincial newspapers, that most frequent
faults in spelling are found. No doubt there
is much to be said which may account for
this. Sometimes their editors are men of
education, aided by a very inefficient staff,
and are at the mercy of their compositors and
readers ; sometimes they are half-educated
men, aspiring to the use of words which they

do not understand. Examples might be gathered of the most absurd mis-spelling and misuse of words, from almost any copy of any provincial journal in the kingdom. In a country newspaper, not long since, I read that a jury might be "*immersed*" in a heavy fine ; the meaning being, of course, that they might be "*amerced.*" We were informed one day last year, in the *Evening Star,* London penny paper, that the Pope went to the "*basilisk*" of St. Peter's ; meaning "*basilica,*" the name given by the Romans to several of their largest churches.

49. How are we to decide between *s* and *z* "*-ize*" or in such words as anathemati*s*e, cauteri*s*e, criti-ci*s*e, deodori*s*e, dogmati*s*e, fraterni*s*e, and the rest ? Many of these are derived from Greek verbs ending in *-izo* ; but more from French verbs ending in *-iser.* It does not seem easy to come to a decision. Usage varies, but has not pronounced positively in any case. It seems more natural to write *anathematize* and *cauterize* with the *z,* but *criticise* is commonly written with the *s.* I remember hearing the late Dr. Donaldson give his opinion that they ought all to be written with *s.* But in the present state of our English usage the question seems an open one.

"show"
and
"shew."

50. It is not easy to say how the verb corresponding to the substantive *show* comes to be spelt *shew*. Here again we seem bound to follow usage, and not rashly to endeavour to reform it.

Pronuncia-
tion—mis-
use of the
aspirate.

51. I pass from spelling to pronunciation. And first and foremost, let me notice that worst of all faults, the leaving out of the aspirate where it ought to be, and putting it in where it ought not to be. This is a vulgarism not confined to this or that province of England, nor especially prevalent in one county or another, but common throughout England to persons of low breeding and inferior education, principally to those among the inhabitants of towns. Nothing so surely stamps a man as below the mark in intelligence, self-respect, and energy, as this unfortunate habit : in intelligence, because, if he were but moderately keen in perception, he would see how it marks him; in self-respect and energy, because if he had these, he would long ago have set to work and cured it. Hundreds of stories are current about the absurd consequences of this vulgarism. We remember in *Punch* the barber who, while operating on a gentleman, expresses his opinion, that, after all, the

cholera was in the *hair.* " Then," observes
the customer, " you ought to be very careful what brushes you use." " Oh, sir," replies
the barber, laughing, "I didn't mean the *air*
of the *ed,* but the *hair* of the *hatmosphere.*"

52. As I write these lines, which I do while
waiting in a refreshment-room at Reading,
between a Great-Western and a South-
Eastern train, I hear one of two commercial
gentlemen, from a neighbouring table, telling
his friend that " his *ed* used to *hake* ready to
burst."

53. The following incident happened at the
house of friends of my own. They had asked
to dinner some acquaintances who were not
perfect in their aspirates. When they made
their appearance somewhat late, imagine the
consternation of my relative, on receiving
from the lady an apology, that she was very
sorry they were after their time, but they
had some *ale* by the way. The well-known
infirmity suggested the charitable explanation, that it was a *storm,* and not a *tipple,*
which had detained them.

54. I had, shortly after the publication of
my first paper in " Good Words," a very
curious communication on the subject of the
pronunciation of the aspirate. My correspon-

dent objected, that the portion of my Essay which treated of this matter conveyed no meaning to him, for that from a child he had never been able to tell the difference in pronunciation between a word beginning with an "*h*," and one beginning without: and he insisted that I ought to have adopted some method of making this plainer. He adds, " In all cases where the ' *h* ' is used, *to me* it appears superfluous." I adduce this without comment, to show how inveterate the habit of neglecting the aspirate must be :—even more so than I had ever imagined.

55. Still, I have known cases where it has been thoroughly eradicated, at the cost, it is true, of considerable pains and diligence. But there are certain words with regard to which the bad habit lingers in persons not otherwise liable to it. We still sometimes, even in good society, hear "*ospital*," "*erb*," and "*umble*,"—all of them very offensive, but the last of them by far the worst, especially when heard from an officiating clergyman. The English Prayer-book has at once settled the pronunciation of this word for us, by causing us to give to God our " *humble* and *hearty* thanks" in the general thanksgiving. *Umble* and *hearty* few can

pronounce without a pain in the throat : and
"*umblanarty*" we certainly never were meant
to say ; *h*umble and *h*earty is the only pronunciation which will suit the alliterative
style of the prayer, which has in it "not only
with our *lips*, but in our *lives*." If it be urged
that we have "*an humble* and contrite heart,"
I answer, so have we "the strength of *an
horse ;*" but no one supposes that we were
meant to say "*a norse.*" The following are
even more decisive : "holy and humble men
of heart :" "*thy* humble servants," not
"*thine.*" It is difficult to believe that this
pronunciation can long survive the satire of
Dickens in David Copperfield : "I am well
aware that I am the umblest person going,"
said Uriah Heep, modestly, "let the other be
who he may. My mother is likewise a very
umble person. We live in a numble abode,
Master Copperfield, but have much to be
thankful for. My father's former calling was
umble ; he was a sexton."

56. As I might have expected, the remarks
here made on the pronunciation of *humble*
have given rise to much controversy. The
unaspirated pronunciation has been stoutly
defended : partly on the ground of being
borrowed from the Italian, partly by the alle-

gation that I have failed to prove from the Prayer-book the intention of the compilers of our Liturgy that the aspirate should be pronounced.

57. It has been asserted by one correspondent that the alliteration in the words, "humble and hearty," is as perfect without the aspirate on the former word, as with it; and I am told that the fact of the occurrence of "*thy humble servants*," and "*thine unworthy servants*," decides nothing, because we have "*thy honour and glory.*" But be it observed, that in order to answer my argument, an instance ought to have been produced, not of a *different* unaspirated vowel with "*thy*" before it, but of the *same* unaspirated vowel; because some vowels have in themselves sounds more or less nearly approaching to the power of a consonant, and therefore enduring "*thy*" and "*a*" before them. The long "*u*" has this power; we may say "*a unit*," "*a university,*" because the first syllable sounds as if it began with "*you*," and "*y*" has here the power of a consonant. But the short "*u*," as in "*humble*," is not one of those vowels which require a consonant to enunciate them: one could not say "*a unlearned man:*" and I

must therefore still maintain that the occurrence of "*thy humble*," and "*thine unworthy*," shows that the "*h*" was meant to be aspirated in the former case, as we know it was not in the latter.

58. Another correspondent brings what is apparently a more formidable objection against my conclusion from "*thy humble*" and "*thine unworthy*." "Were you," he says, "to find the words '*my umbrella*' in some standard work, would you at once exclaim, 'Oh, this writer calls it '*humbrella?*'' Here is an example of the short *u*." My answer is very simple. *Mine* is now almost universally disused: and *my* has taken its place before vowels. The translators of the Bible wrote "*mine eyes:*" but if I found "*my eyes*" in a modern book, I certainly should not charge the writer with aspirating the substantive. I must still maintain that, when the same persons, in the same book, wrote "*thy humble*," and "*thine unworthy*," they meant to indicate a difference, in respect of the aspirate, between the pronunciation of the two words thus differently preceded.

59. Another correspondent, writing from Ireland, charges me with being in error for finding fault with those who drop the aspi-

rate in the word "*hospital*," "for," says he, "no one in *Ireland*, so far as I am aware, ever thinks of aspirating the *h* in that word." This is certainly a curious reason why we should not aspirate it in England. It reminds me of an American friend of ours, who, after spending two or three days with us, ventured to tell us candidly, that we all "*spoke with a strong English accent*." The same correspondent states that he never met an Englishman who could pronounce the relative pronoun "*which*." He charges us all with pronouncing it as if it were "*witch*." I may venture to inform him that it was his ear which was in fault. The ordinary English pronunciation "*which*" is as distinguishable from "*witch*," as it is from the coarse Irish and Scotch "*wh-ich*."

" A " or " an " before a vowel

60. What is our rule—or have we any— respecting the use of *a* or *an* before words beginning with an aspirated *h* ? The rule commonly given is this : that when the accent on the word thus beginning is on the first syllable, we must use *a;* when it is on the second or any following syllable, we may use *an.* This is reasonable enough, because the first syllable, by losing its accent, also loses some portion of the strength of its aspiration.

We cannot aspirate with the same strength the first syllables in the words *history* and *historian*, and in consequence, we commonly say *a history;* but *an historian.*

61. Still, though this may define our modern practice, it is rather a reasonable description of it, than a rule recognised by our best writers. They do not scruple to use *an* before aspirated words, even when the accent falls on the first syllable. In the course of an examination through the letter *h* in the Concordance, verified by the text in all passages which seemed doubtful, I have found in the English version of the Bible very few instances of the article *a* used before a word beginning with *h.* We have *an half, an hammer, an hand, an high hand, an handmaid, an harp, an haven, an head, an heap, an heart, an hedge, an helmet, an help, an herdsman, an heretic, an heritage, an hill, an high hill, an hissing, an holy day, an holy man, an holy angel, an horn, an horrible thing* (I may mention that Cruden has cited *a horrible* in every instance, but that in every instance it stands *an,* both in the edition of 1611 and in our present Bibles), *an horse, an host, an house, an hundred, an husband, an hymn, an hypocrite.* The only exceptions which I have

found are, *a hill*, Josh. xxiv. 33: *a holy solemnity*, Isa. xxx. 29. So that the surprise of a correspondent at Archbishop Trench's having written *an hero* was hardly justified. I do not, of course, mean to say that the usage of the translators of the Bible should be our rule now : but in the absence of any general fixed rule, we can hardly find fault with writers who choose to follow a practice once so widely prevalent, and still kept before the public in the Book most read of all books. I must just remark, that the fact, that we are more particular about this matter than our ancestors were, seems to shew that, notwithstanding the very common vulgarism of dropping the aspirated *h*, the tendency of modern times has been rather to aspirate more, than less.

"Such an one."

62. A correspondent questions the propriety of the common use of "*an*" before "*one*," in the phrase "*such an one.*" I bring this forward not with any idea of deciding it, but because in my examination of the usage of our translators of the Bible, a curious circumstance has come to light. They uniformly used " *such a one*," the expression occurring about thirteen times. In the New Testament, the printers have

altered it throughout to "*such an one:*" in the Old Testament, they have as uniformly left it as it was. It seems to me that we may now, in writing, use either. In common talk, I should always naturally say "*such a one*," not "*such an one*," which would sound formal and stilted.

63. A student at one of our military academies had copied a drawing of a scene in Venice, and in copying the title, had spelt the name of the city *Vennice*. The drawing master put his pen through the superfluous letter, observing, " Don't you know, sir, there is but one *hen* in Venice?" On which the youth burst out laughing. Being asked what he was laughing about, he replied he was thinking *how uncommonly scarce eggs must be there*. The master, in wrath, reported him to the colonel in command, a Scotchman. He, on hearing the disrespectful reply, without in the least perceiving the point of the joke, observed, " An a varra naatural observaation too." *[margin: Only one hen in Venice.]*

64. A worse fault even than dropping the aspirate, is the sounding words ending with *a*, or *aw*, as if they ended with *ar*. A correspondent, accustomed apparently to attend the Houses of Parliament, sends me a strong remonstrance against this practice. He says, *[margin: "Idear," &c.]*

"Woe betide any unfortunate member if he strews the floor with '*aitches*': the laughter is open and merciless: but honourable members may talk of the '*lawrr*' of the land, or '*scawn the idear*,' with perfect impunity. One of the greatest offenders in this matter is a well-known opposition speaker whom I shall not name. The startling way in which he brings out *idear* is enough to make the hair of any one but a well-seasoned Cockney stand on end." My correspondent goes on to say, "*Amelia Ann* is a great stumbling-block to people with this failing, becoming of course in their mouths *Amelia ran*. I remember once seeing a little elementary tract on French pronunciation, in which, opposite the French *a*, was placed *ar*, by way of indicating to British youth the pronunciation thereof. I showed the curiosity to several Londoners, but they could not be made to see the point of the joke."

Calling "u" "oo."

65. There is a very offensive vulgarism, most common in the midland counties, but found more or less almost everywhere: giving what should be the sound of the *u* in certain words, as if it were *oo*: calling "*duty*," *dooty*; "*Tuesday*," *Toosday*; reading to us that "the clouds drop down the *doo*;" exhorting us

"*dooly* to do the *dooties* that are *doo* from us;" asking to be allowed to see the "*noospaper.*" And this is not from incapacity to utter the sound; for though many of these people call "*new,*" *noo,* no one ever yet called "*few,*" *foo;* but it arises from defective education, or from gross carelessness.

66. A Scottish correspondent, speaking of some usages prevalent in the north, says:— "'*Heritor,*' proprietor of landed property, is most commonly pronounced '*eritor,*' which is manifestly inconsistent with '*heritage,* '*hereditary,*' &c., in which the aspiration is always given. In our Scotch courts of law, we hear of entries being made on the '*recórd,*' never *récord :* but in other than law uses the word is always accented on the first syllable. This reminds me of another term in Scotch law— '*Curator,*' pronounced *curător,* in violation, certainly, of the Latin analogy. It is told of a witty Scotch counsel, that when pleading before the House of Lords, and when corrected by one of their lordships for his false quantity in the pronunciation of this word, he replied, with a profound bow, that he must submit to the authority of so learned a *senător,* and so eloquent an *orător.*"

marginal note: "heritor"— "curător."

66*a*. In one letter sent to me, fault is

found with the pronunciations "*decānal*,"
"*ruri-decānal*," "*optātive*," on the ground
that it is the genius of our language always
to throw back the accent to the first syllable of
a tri-syllabic word, as in "*senător*," "*orător*,"
"*minister*." In such a case, custom is our
only guide. It is not to be thought that, because we say "*senător*," "*orător*," or "*minister*," we have any objection to tri-syllabic
words with the accent on the penultima ; we
have hundreds of them : witness "*objector*,"
"*protector*," "*reflector*," "*assertor*," &c. So
that no rule can be laid down, except the
"*norma loquendi*."

"manifold."   67. A correspondent asks for a comment
on the pronunciation of the word "*manifold*."
He thinks that we lose the idea of its original
composition by calling it, as we generally do,
"*mannifold*," and that it ought to be called
"*many-fold*," as if it were two words. My
reply would be, that the end proposed is a
praiseworthy one, but I am afraid it will
not justify the means used in attaining it—
viz., the violation of common usage, which
has stamped "*mannifold*" with its approval.
It may be that the mispronunciation first originated in the apparent analogy with "*manifest*." I would remind him, that this is not

the only word which suffers change of pronunciation when compounded. We call a "*vine-yard*," "*vinyard :*" the man would be deservedly set down as a pedant who should do otherwise. We call a "*cup-board*" a "*cubbard*," a "*half-penny*" a "*haepny*," and we similarly contract many other compound words. The great rule, I take it, in all such cases of conventional departure from the pronunciation of words as spelt, is to do nothing which can attract attention. We naturally think somewhat less favourably than we otherwise should of a person who says "*victu-al*," when the rest of the world say "*vittal ;*" "*med-i-cine*," when others say "*med'cine ;*" "*ve-ni-son*," where we thought we should hear "*ven'son*." We commonly expect that such a man will be strong-willed, and hard to deal with in ordinary life : and I think we are not often wrong.

68. A correspondent complains of the stress "prophecy." laid on the final syllable of the substantive *prophecȳ :* and says, "What should we think of *ecstasȳ, fallacȳ, phantasȳ,* especially if put in the plural ? " But in this case, usage is right, and apparent analogy wrong. *Ecstasy,* as we have already seen, is from the Greek *ecstasis ; phantasy,* from the Greek *phantasia ;*

fallacy, from the Latin *fallacĭa*. But *pro-prhecy* is from the Greek *propheteīa :* and it is therefore not without reason that we lay the stress on the last syllable. The verb, *to pro-phesy*, we pronounce in the same way ; I sup-pose, by a double analogy : partly guided by the sound of the substantive, partly by that of the last syllable in other verbs ending in " *y*," to qualif$\bar{y}$, to amplify, to mystif$\bar{y}$, &c.

"alms," &c.   69. Complaint has been made of the pro-nunciation of the words *alms, psalms, calm*, after the fashion of *elm* and *film*. No doubt the marked utterance of the " *l*" in these words would savour of affectation ; at the same time, there is a subdued sound of it which should be heard in " *alms :*" even less audibly in " *psalm*," and hardly at all in " *calm :*" usage, as learnt in society, being in this, as in other uncertain pronunciations, the only safe guide.

"Cowper."   70. There are two words, the pronunciation of the former of which can easily be settled, whereas that of the latter seems to defy all settlement. How are we to call the Christian poet who spells his name *C-o-w-p-e-r ?* He himself has decided this for us. He makes his name rhyme with *trooper*. We must therefore call him *Coo-per*, not *Cow-per ;*

seeing that a man's own usage is undeniably
the rule for the pronunciation of his own
name. I have had a letter from a correspondent, urging that this rhyme may have been
only a poetical pronunciation of the name, not
the usual one ; as Coleridge in one place
makes his name rhyme to "polar ridge." But
I have received an interesting testimony from
Dr. Goddard Rogers, confirming the settlement of the pronunciation as given above.
" Cowper," he says, " not only decided the
matter by 'making his name rhyme to trooper;'
but in conversation always begged his friends
to call him Cooper. I have this from a very
old gentleman whom I attended in his last
illness. He was Thomas Palmer Bull, son of
Cowper's friend, ' smoke-inhaling Bull,' and
had himself heard the poet make the remark."

71. Another word also brings into ques- "cucum-
tion the "*coo*" and "*cow*," but without any
such chance of a settlement. It is the agreeable but somewhat indigestible gourd spelt
c-u-c-u-m-b-e-r. Is it to be *coo*-cumber? *cow*-
cumber? or *kew*-cumber? The point is one
warmly debated : so warmly in certain circles,
that when I had a house full of pupils, we
were driven to legislation on it, merely to
keep the peace of the household. Whenever

the unfortunate word occurred at table, which was almost every day during the summer months, a fierce fray invariably set in. At last we abated the nuisance by enacting that in future the first syllable should be dropped, and the article be called for under the undebateable name of "*cumber*." Perhaps, of the three, the strongest claim might be set up for *kew*, or *Q-cumber* : seeing that the Latin name, *cucumis*, can hardly by English lips be otherwise pronounced.

Mis-pro-nunciation of Scripture names.

72. I cannot abstain from saying a few words on the mispronunciation of Scripture proper names by our clergy. This, let me remind them, is quite inexcusable. It shows a disregard and absence of pains in a matter, about the least part of which no pains ought to be spared. To take it on no other ground, is it justifiable in them to allow themselves to offend by their ignorance or carelessness the ears of the most intelligent of their hearers ? This was not the spirit of one who said he would not eat meat while the world lasted, if it scandalized his neighbour. But this is not all. When I hear a man flounder about among St. Paul's salutations, calling half of them wrongly, I am sure that that man does not know his Bible. The same

carelessness is sure to show itself in misappropriation of texts, wrong understanding of obsolete phrases, and the like. The man who talks of Aristobŭlus in the Lesson, is as likely as not to preach from St. Paul's " I know nothing by myself," to show us that the Apostle *wanted divine teaching,* and not to be aware that he meant, *he was not conscious of any fault.**

73. Three Sundays before this was written, Examples. Jan. 18, 1863, we had the crucial chapter, Rom. xvi., for the evening lesson. A friend writes to me from a distant city in Italy :— " In the afternoon a stranger officiated ; but as he saluted *As*syncrītus and Patrōbas, I knew what to expect in the sermon, and so it was." Another writes from London, that he was on that day at a fashionable London church, and heard Epenētus and Patrōbas introduced to the congregation. A clergyman in the West of England found on his breakfast-table one Monday morning a note from his congregation to this effect :—

> To-day you said, " ye know Stephānas ;"
> This misconception, sir, doth pain us :
> For it is Stephānas we know,
> And beg that you will call him so.†

---

* See the text explained, in paragraph 319 below.

† I have had a very amusing letter, written anony-

A friend of mine heard the following in a London church, and, strange to say, from a schoolmaster :—"Trophīmus have I left at Milĕtum sick." But it perhaps may be said to me, with the beautiful inconsequence of the logic of the present day, Is a man a perfect Christian minister, because he knows how to pronounce these names? To which I fearlessly answer, "No, by no means ; but he is, at all events, as near to it as if he did not know how to pronounce them." I am put in mind, by this question, of "Johnny Stittle," a redoubtable preacher who used to hold forth at Cambridge, in a chapel in Green Street. The tradition of him and his sayings was yet a living thing, when I went up as an under-graduate in 1828. His wont was to rail at the studies of the University ; and in doing so on one occasion, after having wound himself up to the requisite pitch of fervour, he exclaimed, in a

"Johnny Stittle."

mously, from the clergyman in the West of England to whom these verses were sent. He comes to a rather curious conclusion from the fact of my having told the story. He infers that I was present, and that I made the verses. As this may be my only means of communicating with him, let me assure him this was not the case. I merely tell the tale as 'twas told to me.

voice of thunder, "D'ye think *Powl* knew Greek?"*

74. A writer in the "English Churchman"

* I have had two interesting communications from Cambridge, giving accurate details respecting "Johnny Stittle."

He is mentioned in the Rev. Abner Brown's "Recollections of Rev. Chas. Simeon," Introduction, p. xiii., where he is described as a "day labourer," and it is said that Mr. Simeon thought well enough of him to encourage him by pecuniary assistance.

In a memoir of Rowland Hill, by Mr. Jones, are the following notices of Stittle:—

"During Mr. Hill's residence at Cambridge he was much attached to 'Johnny Stittle,' one of Mr. Berridge's converts. He was naturally a gifted man, though, like his patron, he moved in his own orbit. He preached for many years in Green Street, Cambridge, and died in 1813, in his 87th year.

"As Mr. Hill was on his way to Duxford to preach for the Missionary Society, he suddenly exclaimed, 'I must go to Cambridge, and see the widow of an old clergyman who is living there, for I have a message to leave with her.' On being asked if the message was important, he replied, 'Yes, sir, I want the old lady—who will soon be in heaven—to give my love to Johnny Stittle, and to tell him I shall soon see him again.'"

Another correspondent says, "I am old enough to remember, and to have actually heard, Johnny Stittle at Cambridge. He compared eternity, in one of his sermons, to a great clock, which said 'tick' in one century, and 'tack' in the next. Then suddenly turning to some gownsmen, he said, 'Now go home, and calculate the length of the pendulum."

One must acknowledge that if there was eccentricity here, there was something very like genius also.

adds the following to many instances of mispronunciation of Scripture proper names.
"Too well," says the writer in the "Churchman," "do I remember the city of *Colossé*
pronounced *Coloss*, as if it were a word of
only two syllables; *the epistle to Philĕmon;*
'*the gainsaying of Core*' (one syllable), betray-
ing that the speaker had no conception he
was talking of the person who in the 16th
chapter of Numbers is designated 'Korah.'"
I have also a complaint sent me of a clergyman who insists on always saying "*Achaĭcus;*"
and an anecdote of a remark being made, how
well the *Venĭte exultĕmus* was chanted.

75. A correspondent requests me to endeavour to correct the very common mispronunciation Timothēus, into the proper sound,
Timothĕ-ŭs. On the other hand, one of my
Censors expresses a hope that as I so strongly
advocate our following the Greeks in the pronunciation of their proper names, I shall be
consistent, and never again, in reading the
lessons, call those ancient cities, Samaria and
Philadelphia, otherwise than *Samarīa* and
Philadelphīa. The answer to this is very
simple—viz., that I do not advocate the
following of the Greeks in the pronunciation
of their proper names, in any case where

Samarīa
and Phila-
delphīa.

English usage has departed from their pronunciation. It is in cases where there is no
such usage, and where the reader is thrown
back on what ought to be his own knowledge
of the form and composition of the name, that
we are pained at discovering that one who
ought to be able rightly to divide the Word
of Truth, is not in the habit of consulting his
New Testament in the original Greek.

76. But there is more to be said about the
two rather unfortunate instances given by my
critic. The tendency of our language has
been universally to shorten the last syllable
but one, in those names of cities which in
Greek ended in *ĭa*. *Alexandrĭa* is now called
Alexandrīa ; Seleucĭa, Seleucīa ; and *Samarĭa*
and *Philadelphĭa, Samarīa* and *Philadelphīa.*
But no such usage infringes the proper Greek
pronunciation of *Epænĕtus, Asyncrĭtus, Patrŏ-
bas, Aristobūlus,* and the like. Of course,
usage is not immutable. We now say *Zabŭ-
lon,* but the day may come when the stricter
scholars may have overborne common usage,
and we may say *Zabūlon,* which is right
according to the Hebrew and the Greek. We
now say *Sennachĕrib;* and so universal is this
usage, that a correspondent writes in strong
terms, stigmatising the strictly accurate pro-

nunciation, *Sennachĕrib*, as a blunder.   When
I was at school, the common practice was to
pronounce the names of two of the Greek
letters, as "*Epsĭlon*," and "*Omĭcron:*" now,
such sounds are unknown in schools, and the
right pronunciation, "*Epsīlon*" and "*Omīcron*,"
is universal.

Urbane.   77. Three correspondents have written
about another Scripture name.   It is that of
a person saluted in Rom. xvi. 9, and in
our present Bibles spelt *U-r-b-a-n-e*.   The
common idea respecting this name is that it
belongs to a woman, and most readers pronounce it as three syllables, *Urbānê*.   But it
is simply the English for the Latin name
Urbanus, in English *Urbane*, or, as we now
call it, *Urban*.   The assumed name of the
Editor of "The Gentleman's Magazine" has
been, time out of mind, Sylvanus Urban.
The royal printers, who have made so many
unauthorised alterations in the text of our
Bibles, might with advantage drop out the
final "*e*" from this word, and thus prevent
the possibility of confusion.

Junias.   78. I may mention that in verse 7 of the
same chapter, *Junia*, who is mentioned with
Andronicus, is not a woman, but a man,
Junias.

79. While treating of the pronunciation of "covetous." those who minister in public, two other words occur to me which are very commonly mangled by our clergy. One of these is "*covetous*," and its substantive, "*covetousness*." I hope that some of my clerical readers will be induced to leave off pronouncing them "*covetious*," and "*covetiousness*." I can assure them, that when they do thus call the words, one at least of their hearers has his appreciation of their teaching disturbed.

80. The other hint I would venture to give the Revelation. them is, that the mysterious concluding book of Scripture is the *Revelation** of St. John, not the *Revelations*. I imagine this very common mistake must have arisen from our being accustomed to speak of the Lamenta*tions* of Jeremiah, in which case the word *is plural*.

80*a*. A complaint respecting slovenly pro- "Able" for "Abel," &c. nunciation has been sent me, which seems to bring before us a matter of some delicacy and uncertainty. A correspondent blames

---

* I had a strong letter of remonstrance for having called this book the "*Revelation of St. John*," where-as it is, by ch. i. 1, "the Revelation of Jesus Christ." Here we have a misapprehension of the meaning of the preposition; so puerile, as not to be worth recording, were it not to illustrate a point hereafter to be treated of.

rightly the slovenly habit of pronouncing
" Abel," " Mabel," " Ethel," as if they were
" *Able*," " *Mable*," " *Ethle* ;" and speaks
with proper severity of Walker, who, in his
" Pronouncing Dictionary," has set down
" *evle*," as the pronunciation of " evil." So
far seems clear. But, when we come to
the question, whether all words in *-el* or *-il*
are to be rigidly pronounced in full, we are,
I think, compelled to yield somewhat to
custom. Nay, custom has, as matter of fact,
prevailed in some cases, even to the alteration of our conventional spelling. What was
once " battail," then " battel," has now become " battle ;" " chattail,". or " chattel,"
has become " cattle ;" " subtile," or " sub-
til," has become " subtle ;" " castell," or
" castel," has become " castle." The word
" devil" is far more frequently pronounced
" devvle," than " de-vill ;" indeed, this latter
pronunciation, in the mouth of an affected
precisian, is offensive. Good taste, and the
observance of usage, must in such matters
be our guides.

Criticism in a news-paper.

81. A very curious and choice bit of
newspaper criticism on these "notes" was
sent me the other day. The writer says :
" There seems, to our mind, something small,

not to say ludicrous and absurd, about the
notion of a dignitary of the Church of England constituting himself the censor and
reporter of small slips of pronunciation, such
as *Sophœnētus* for *Sophœnĕtus*, and the like.
We should think none the worse of a man for
tripping once, or even twice, in those long
Pauline lists of salutations. Not to trip at
all would, except in the case of practised and
familiar scholars, suggest to us the notion
that rather more pains and time had been
bestowed upon the matter than it deserved."
Where this critic found the name *Sophœnetus*
among the Pauline salutations, I am at a loss
to say : at all events it shews that he practised his own advice, and had not bestowed
more time nor pains on the matter than it
deserved. But it is his doctrine, that in
knowledge of the proprieties of these minute
points in Scripture, inaccuracy is better than
accuracy, that I would especially hold up
for reprobation. Very little time and pains
are really required in the matter. Every
clergyman is, or ought to be, familiar with his
Greek Testament : two minutes' reference to
that will show him how every one of these
names ought to be pronounced ; or if he is in
the practice of regular reading in the original,

F

he will not want even this two minutes' reference. And those who cannot refer to the original will be kept right without any pains at all, if the clergy are right; for they will simply follow their leaders. Surely this doctrine of the writer in the newspaper cannot represent the general opinion among those bodies who have of late years been making such remarkable advance in the accurate study of the original text of the Scriptures, and have by the results of the training in some of their admirable colleges done so much for the credit of biblical scholarship in England.

82. For my own part, I was disposed to put together this critique and a letter which I received from a friend, saying that he had heard a person, not a clergyman, read *Arctŭrus* and *Orĭon* and the *Pleiādes.* I could not help imagining that I had tracked my critic *tripping twice or even more* in what I daresay he believes to be some more of these Pauline salutations.*

Serious accompaniments of ignorance in this matter.

83. The really serious aspect of the matter comes before us, when we hear what my friend adds, that the man thus reading proceeded to *expound the chapter.* An error in pronuncia-

* See note B at end of book.

tion may be, in an ordinary person, a trifle; but when a *teacher* makes it, it is no longer a trifle: and for this reason, that a teacher is bound to be acquainted with the real meaning of that which he expounds, and enforces; with the context of the passages, and with the spirit and force of the sacred word as the Spirit has given it to us. And when we find a teacher ignorant of even outward matters of common information respecting the text, we are not led to hope much for his power of rightly dividing the word of truth. That it may please Him who is the fountain of wisdom, to make exceptions, and to endow even ignorant men with insight into the meaning of His word, no one would deny; still, it is not our business to take such exceptions for granted, but rather to take for granted His ordinary course of proceeding on our part, and to provide for its success as we best may. He who feels this, will not think correctness even in the lists of Pauline salutations a trifling matter.

84. I now come to that which must form a principal part of my little work,—some notes on the usage of words and construction of sentences. And let me premise, in order to prevent mistakes, that my object in these

Usage and construction.

notes is not to lay down nor to exemplify
mere rules of grammar,—though of course
the consideration of such rules must often
come before us,—but to illustrate the usages
and tendencies of our common language, as
matter of fact, by the discussion of questions
arising out of doubtful words and phrases.
One of the most interesting subjects connected
with a language is its tendencies: the currents, so to speak, which set in for or against
certain modes of speech or thought. These
are to be discovered in all languages, and in
none more notably than our own. We are a
mixed race, and our tongue everywhere bears
traces of the fact. We have gone through
more crises of religious and political strife
than most nations, and thought and speech
have ever been freer in England than in
other countries. From these, and from other
circumstances, the English language has become more idiomatic than most others; and
the tendency is still going on among us, to
set aside accurate grammatical construction,
and to speak rather according to idiom than
according to rule.

Idiom.   85. Let me explain myself: and to this
end let me say something about that which is
known as the *idiom* of a language, as distin-

guished from strictness of grammatical construction. This word "idiom," then, is derived from the Greek, and properly signifies a thing or habit peculiar to one person or set of persons, and forming an exception to general rules. Our usage of the term has confined this its meaning in English to matters of *language.* When we speak of an idiom, we mean some saying, or some way of speaking, peculiar to some one language or family of languages, which can only be accounted for by the peculiar tendency, or habit of thought, of those who use it. When we say that a phrase is *idiomatic,* we mean that it bears this character.

86. Now let us see to what this amounts. Such expressions, if judged by strict rules, will commonly fail to satisfy them. In so far as they are idiomatic, they are departures from the beaten track of that grammatical construction, and that critical analogy, which are common to all languages. For the rules of grammar and of logic, being dependent not on local usage, but on the constitution of the human mind, are common to all nations. And when any nation sets up, so to speak, for itself, and indulges in the peculiarities which we call idioms, it

takes a course which these general rules do not justify.

87. Let us show this by some examples. It is the habit of modern European nations to avoid the second person singular in addressing individuals. Some languages use the second person plural instead : some the third person. The English, the French, and others, say "*you*" for "*thou :*" the Germans, and those cognate to them, say "*they*" for "*thou :*" the Italians, still more strangely, say "*she*," meaning "your excellency." These are the *idioms* or *idiomatic usages* of these languages respectively. Every one speaking any of those languages must use the idiomatic expression, or he would render himself ridiculous. *

* Nay, the consequences may sometimes be much more serious. A correspondent sends me the following story : "My friend, a student in the University of Heidelberg, acquired his first knowledge of German chiefly by colloquial exercise with his fellow-students, who habitually addressed each other in the second person singular, '*du*.' Having thus acquired enough of the language to blunder through a conversation, he was present at a party, where he danced with the sister of one of his fellow-students, and entertained her with the choicest German at his command, but unfortunately always addressed her as '*du*.' This (to a German ear) impertinent familiarity was either overheard by, or reported to, the young lady's brother, who deemed it impossible to wipe out the scandal by any other means

88. But, if we judge such expressions by strict rules, they cannot be defended. It cannot be correct to address one person as if he were many : it cannot be correct to look at and address one person as if he were not present, and, being absent, were more than one. We all know this : notwithstanding we do not criticise and carp at every such usage, but simply acquiesce in it as being the common custom.

89. Let us take another instance. Some languages are more *elliptic* than others : that is, the habits of thought of some nations will bear the omission of certain members of a sentence, better than the habits of thought of other nations. In English we should say, "*At the Equinox the sun rises at six and sets at six.*" But if we were speaking in French, we should say, "At the Equinox, the sun rises at six hours of the morning, and sets at six hours of the evening." Now here there is

Elliptic usages.

than a duel. In vain my friend explained his ignorance of the German conventional mode of address. The offence had been committed in public, and if the culprit wished to remain at Heidelberg in peace in future, he must fight there. They fought accordingly, and the skilful German cleverly inflicted a slight wound which drew blood ; honour was satisfied, and the affair ended in pipes, friendship, and beer."

no doubt that the Frenchman has the advantage in fulness and propriety of expression. Any one disposed to cavil at our English sentence, and to treat it as some of my sentences have been treated, might say, "rises at six and sets at six! Six what? Six miles, or six minutes, or six occasions?" But we do not in practice thus cavil, because we are in the enjoyment of common sense, and we are prepared, in the daily use of our language, to omit that which the thought would naturally supply.*

Caprice of idiom.

90. One more example. In English, our common mode of salutation to one another is, "*How d'ye do?*" Now of course we all understand, that in this phrase we use the verb "*do*" in a neuter sense : in the same sense which it bears in the reply of the disciples concerning Lazarus : "Lord, if he sleep, he shall do well." But suppose a person were to insist on this usage being carried throughout our converse, and to make it an objection to the question "*How d'ye do?*" that one cannot say in the same sense, "I went to see A or B, and he *did well.*" We should at once reply, if we thought on the matter, that while

---

* See note C, at the end of the volume.

the verb admits of being thus used in certain
tenses, and in certain connexions, it does not
admit of being thus used in certain other
tenses, and in certain other connexions ; and
that the account to be given of this is, that
the English people will have it so : it is an
idiom, or arbitrary usage, of their language.

91. The capricious character of idiomatic
usage is admirably illustrated by this very
example. For though it is admissible to say,
" I went to see A or B, and he was doing very
well," the words would not carry the sense,
that I was able to say to him " How d'ye
do ?" and he to reply, " Very well, thank
you;" but would convey the impression that
he had lately met with an accident, and was
going on favourably.

92. Some idiomatic expressions seem to "methinks.
defy any attempt to give a satisfactory account of them. Take the phrase " *methinks.*"
It is believed to have arisen from a strange
impersonal use of the verb, and the transposition of the pronoun, which should come
after it. We have the simlar phrase, " *me-
seems,*" which can more easily be resolved :
viz., into " it seems to me." That this is the
account to be given of both, appears plain,
seeing that in both cases we find in use the

other and more formal third person, "*me-thinketh*" and "*me-seemeth*." But what an expression to come under the ferule of the strict grammarian !

Example from the Greek.

93. I want yet one more example for the purpose I have in view, and I must get it from a dead language. In the Greek,—which is perhaps the finest and most subtle vehicle ever formed for human thought,—it is the practice to join a plural noun of the neuter gender to a verb in the singular number. Now, of course, according to the rules of universal grammar, this is wrong. A plural noun should be joined to a plural verb. But the Greek had his reason, and a very good one it was. He felt, that things without life, when spoken of in the plural, formed but one mass, and might be treated as one thing. And so the tendency of the national thought, which was to define and to express the subtle distinctions of thought, prevailed over the rule of grammar, and the usage became idiomatic.

Spoken and written English.

94. Let another thing also be remembered. We must distinguish between the English which we speak, and that which we write. Many expressions are not only tolerated but required in conversation, which are

not usually put on paper. Thus, for instance, everyone says "*can't*" for *cannot*, "*won't*" for *will not*, "*isn't*" for *is not*, in conversation; but we seldom see these contractions in books, except where a conversation is related. This is a difference which the foreigner is generally slow in apprehending. He says "*I will not*," "*I cannot*," "*I must not*," "*I shall not*:" "*I am*," for "*I'm*," "*they are*" for "*they're*:" and he often may be detected by his precision in these matters, even after he has mastered the pronunciation and construction of our language. This difference between our spoken and our written language should always be borne in mind, when we are treating of expressions commonly found in colloquial English. Many persons, in judging of them, bring them to the test of the stricter rule of written composition, to which they are not fairly amenable.

95. Let me further illustrate this tendency of nations by another usage now almost become idiomatic, and commonly found in the talk of us all. I mean the expression "*these*" or "*those kind of things.*" At first sight, this seems incorrect and indefensible. It would appear as if we ought to say "*this kind of things*," "*that kind of things.*" It

"those kind of things."

becomes then an interesting inquiry, as it was in the other case, why this should be so. And here again my readers must excuse me if I go to a dead language for my illustration —not for my *reason:* the *reason* will be found in the laws of thought : but it will be best illustrated by citing the usage of that language in which, more than in any other, the laws of thought have found their expression.

" attrac-
tion."

96. In the Greek language, there is an idiomatic usage called *attraction.* It may be thus described. If an important noun in a sentence is in a certain case, say the genitive or dative, a relative pronoun referring to it is put in the same case, though by the construction of the sentence it ought to be in another. Thus, if I wanted to put into Greek the sentence, "*I gave it to the man whom I saw,*" the relative pronoun "*whom*" would not be in the accusative case, as it ought to be, governed by the verb " *saw,*" but in the same case as "*man,*" viz., dative, and the sentence would be roughly represented, as far as the mere form of it is concerned, by the English " *I gave it to the man, to whom I saw.*"

97. Now in the way of speaking of which I treat, it is evident that this same tendency, to draw the less important word into simi-

larity to the more important one, is suffered to prevail over strict grammatical exactness. We are speaking of "*things*" in the plural. Our pronoun "*this*" really has reference to "*kind*," not to "*things;*" but the fact of "*things*" being plural, gives a plural complexion to the whole, and we are tempted to put "*this*" into the plural. That this is the account to be given, appears still more plainly from the fact that not unfrequently we find a rival attraction prevails, and the clause takes a *singular* complexion from the other substantive, "*kind.*" We often hear people say, "*this kind of thing,*" "*that sort of thing.*" It must be confessed that the phrases, "*this kind of things,*" "*that sort of things,*" have a very awkward sound; and we find that our best writers have the popular expression, *These kind, those sort.**

98. One word on "*this*" and "*that*," as we pass onward. "*This*" and "*these*" refer to persons and things *present*, or under immediate consideration; "*that*" and "*those*" to persons and things *not present*, nor under immediate consideration; or if either of these, one degree further removed than the others

"this" and "that."

---

* See note D, at the end of the volume.

of which are used "*this*" and "*these*." We find this rule sometimes curiously violated in conversation and in writing. A barrister tells me that the confusion is common in the Irish law courts : "Those arguments I now use," &c. Another Irish correspondent is often greeted with, "That's a could day, yer riv'rence." I have a Scottish friend, who always designates the book which he has in his hand as "*that book;*" the portfolio of drawings which he is turning over as "*those drawings.*"

99. We have this usage in England, but it carries another meaning. If I have a book in my hand, and say, "*that book will make a great sensation,*" I mean to remove my own and my hearer's attention from the particular volume, or even the present consideration of its contents, and to describe it in its general, and as it were historical, effect on the world.

100. The oddest departure from the common usage of "*this*" and "*that*," which I remember to have observed, was in a notice which I repeatedly saw, in the summer of 1863, posted on houses in Devonshire, "*Those houses to let,*" "*That house for sale.*"

100*a*. In "*this day*," "*this night*," the

"to-day," "to-night."

somewhat stiff and formal demonstrative pronoun is curiously abbreviated. " *To-day*," " *to-night*," are universally used. In the dialect of the western counties, " *this year*," is commonly expressed by " *to-year*." In Scotland and Ireland, " *the day*," " *the night*," " *the year*," are the ordinary expressions : " it'll no rain the day," &c.

101. Confusion sometimes arises in our language from the triple meaning of " *that*," which, with us, is a demonstrative pronoun, a relative pronoun, and a conjunction. It is possible to use six " *thats*" consecutively in the same sentence. Take the sentence, "He said, that the meaning which the report which that man told him had been thought to bear was more than had been intended." Here I have already " *that*," conjunction ; and I may express " *the meaning*," by " *that*," demonstrative pronoun ; " *which*," by " *that*," relative pronoun ; " *the report*," by " *that*," demonstrative pronoun ; " *which*" again, by " *that*," relative pronoun ; and then I end with " *that man*," " *that*" being in this last case again a demonstrative pronoun. So that I get the following sentence, with, as I said, six " *thats*" occurring consecutively : " He said, *that that that that that that* man told him had been

Triple meaning of "that."

thought to mean, was more than had been intended." *

102. From this threefold import of the word it sometimes is not apprehended which of its meanings it bears in a given sentence. Ps. xc. 4, in the Prayer-book version runs thus —" A thousand years in Thy sight are but as yesterday, *seeing that is past as a watch in the night.*" Here, of course, *that* is the demonstrative pronoun, and refers to "*yesterday,*" which has just been spoken of; and it ought, in reading, to have a certain emphasis laid on it. But not unfrequently we hear it read in the responses of the congregation, as if it were the conjunction: "Seeing thăt is past as a watch in the night." I remember having some trouble in curing our choristers at Canterbury of singing it thus.

"this much," "that much."

103. What are we to think of the very common expressions, "*this much,*" "*that much?*" We continually hear and read, "*This much* I know," "Of *that much* I am

---

* *Seven "thats"* may be used together, if one of them is a mere *citation.* "I assert *that that* 'that,' *that that that that* person told me contained, was improperly emphasized." And this use may be carried even further yet: "I assert, *that that, that that* 'that,' *that that that that* person told me contained, implied, has been misunderstood."

certain," and the like. It might be supposed
at first sight that this way of speaking was
indefensible. "*Much*" is an adjective of
quantity, and requires, in order to define it,
not a pronoun, but an adverb. We may say
very much, pretty much (where "*pretty*" is
used in its colloquial adverbial sense of
tolerably, moderately), *as much, so much,* or
thus much; but from such a view it would
appear that we must not say "*this much,*" or
"*that much.*" Still, may not another view
be taken? High, deep, long, broad, are
adjectives of measure; but we may say *a
foot high, a yard long, an ell broad.* And if
we choose to designate with the hand, or
otherwise, the measure of a foot, yard, or ell,
we may substitute the demonstrative pronoun
for the substantive, and say with precisely
the same construction of the sentence, "*this
high,*" "*this long,*" "*that broad.*" Now, how
is this with "*much?*" If I may use *this* and
that to point out the extent of length, height,
and breadth which I want to indicate, why
not also to point out the extent of *quantity*
which I want to indicate? When I say "*Of
this much I am certain,*" I indicate, by the pronoun *this,* something which I am about to
state, and which is the extent of my cer-

tainty. When I say "*That much I knew
before*," I indicate, by the pronoun "*that*," the
piece of intelligence which my friend supposed
to be new to me. But it may be replied, I
might have said, "*Of this I am certain*,"
"*That I knew before.*" True: but then I
should express nothing as to *the extent* of my
certainty or previous knowledge. I believe
both expressions to be correct; not so elegant
perhaps as "*Thus much*," but at the same
time more fitted for colloquial use.

"that ill."   104. There is one use of *that*, which is quite
indefensible, and, indeed, is not found except as
a provincialism. I mention it, because some
might suppose that what I have said might
be cited in defence of it likewise. I mean,
when it is used as a qualifying word with
adjectives not denoting extent, and when
itself must be explained by "*to that extent.*"
I have heard in the midland and eastern
counties, "I was *that ill*, that I could not go
to work:" "He was *that drunk*, that he
didn't know what he was about."*

"ever so"
or "never
so?".   105. Are we to say "*ever so*," or "*never so*,"
in expressions like "be he *ever* (*never*) so old,"

---

* An Irish correspondent informs me that "*which?*"
is used in Ireland as equivalent to our "*what?*" or
"*what did you say?*"

and the like? Usage seems divided. In familiar speech we mostly say "*ever so:*" in writing, and especially in the solemn and elevated style, we mostly find "*never so.*" We say to a troublesome petitioner, "If you ask me *ever* so much, I won't give it you:" but we read, "Which refuseth to hear the voice of the charmer, charm he *never* so wisely." Can we give any account of this? What is the difference between the expressions? Because one would think there must be some difference, when two such words are concerned, which are the very opposites of one another. Sentences similarly constructed with these two words are as different in meaning as possible. "Had he *ever* loved at all," and "Had he *never* loved at all," are opposite in meaning to one another. And so, actually and literally, are the two which we are now considering: but in the general sense they both convey the meaning which is intended. This may be made plain as follows: "Be it *ever* so large,' means, "though it attain every imaginable degree of size:" "be it *never* so large," means, "though there be no imaginable degree of size which it does not attain." The former is inclusively affirmative; the latter is exclusively negative : and these two amount to the same.

"what was," "what was not."

106. There are some curious phenomena coming under the same head as this last. I may say, "What was my astonishment," and I may say, "What was not my astonishment," and I may convey the same meaning. By the former I mean, "how great was my astonishment ;" by the latter, that no astonishment could be greater than mine was.

"no" and "yes" the same.

107. Another correspondent mentions a curious fact about negatives and affirmatives. If we were to ask the question, "Had you only the children with you?" a person south of the Tweed would answer "*no*," and a person north of the Tweed "*yes*," both meaning the same thing—viz., that only the children were there. I think I should myself, though a Southron, answer *yes*. But there is no doubt that such questions are answered in the two ways when the same meaning is intended to be conveyed. The account to be given of this seems to be, that "only" is "none but." "Had you none but the children with you?" and the answer is "*None*," affirming the question. So that the negative form naturally occurs to the mind in framing its answer, and "*none*" becomes "*no*." Whereas in the other

case this form does not occur to the mind, but simply to affirm the matter inquired of, viz., the having only the children : and the answer is " *Even so*," or " *Yes.*"

108. In some sentences unobjectionably " oldest inmate." expressed, it is impossible to be sure of the meaning. An establishment has been founded fifty years. A person tells me that he is "one of its oldest inmates." Am I to understand that he is one of the few survivors of those who came to it at or near its first foundation, in which case he may be any age above fifty ; or am I to understand that he is at the present moment one of the oldest in age of the inmates there, which would bring his age up to between eighty and ninety ? In other words, does the term "*oldest*" qualify him absolutely, or only as an inmate of that establishment ?

109. The mention of degrees of compa- " lesser." rison leads me to another point, which I have been requested to notice by more than one correspondent. It is the use of *lesser* in certain combinations, instead of *less*. Are we to stigmatise this as an impropriety, or to regard it as an idiomatic irregularity which we must be content to tolerate ? It seems to me that the latter must be our course.

The usage is sanctioned by our best writers, and that not here and there, but uniformly. " God made two great lights : the greater light to rule the day, and the *lesser* light to rule the night."

110. The account to be given of it seems to be somewhat like that which we gave of a former irregularity : that it has arisen originally by the force of attraction to another word, *greater*, which in such sentences precedes it. For example, when we have spoken of " *the greater light*," " *the less light*" sounds halting and imperfect ; and the termination *er* is added to balance the sentence. Sometimes the usage occurs where the other word is not expressed : as when we say " the *lesser* of two evils :" but still the comparison is in the mind, though not on the tongue. It may be too, that it is not only the sound of the one word " *greater*," which is usually the companion of " *lesser*," but that of almost every other comparative in the language, which has produced the effect ; for they are almost without exception dissyllables. It is a confirmation of the account which we have been giving of this usage, that no one thinks of attaching the additional syllable to " *less* " when it is combined

with "*more;*" *more and less* being already well balanced.

111. We may notice the growing practice "replace." of using the word "*replace,*" to signify just the opposite of its real meaning. " Lord Derby went out of office, and *was replaced* by Lord Palmerston." This, as *now* used, conveys the meaning, "*was succeeded by* Lord Palmerston." But put the sentence before our grandfathers, and they would have understood it to mean that Lord Derby went out of office, and Lord Palmerston *put him in again;* he was *replaced* by Lord Palmerston.

112. I need not say that the usage is borrowed from that of the French "*remplacer.*" But there is this difference, that the French verb does not mean to *replace,* in our sense, nor has it in its derivation anything to do with "*replace,*" but is "*remplir la place,*" "*to fill the place,*" and thus has for its proper meaning that which it is now attempted to give the English word *replace.* Lord Derby went out of office, and was "*remplacé,*" i.e., *his place was filled,* by Lord Palmerston ; but he was not *replaced,* i.e., *put back again,* by his rival.

113. The "*enclosure*" of a letter, what is " enclosure." it ? Is it that which *encloses* the letter, viz.,

the envelope ? or is it something *enclosed in* the letter, as a dried flower, or a lock of hair ? or is it something *enclosed with* the letter, as another letter of the same size, or a map or plan of a larger size ?

114. Strictly speaking, I suppose the noun is an abstract one, signifying *the act of enclosing*, as *exposure* means *the act of exposing*. In this sense we might say "the *enclosure* of letters in envelopes, before the penny postage was established, incurred the payment of double postage." Then, when we pass from the abstract to the concrete use of the word, *i.e.*, use it to signify not the act of enclosing, but something which is the instrument, or object, or result of that act, the question arises, ought it to signify the thing *enclosing*, or the thing *enclosed* ? There are examples both ways. *Cincture* is properly the act of girding. *A cincture* is the thing which girds, not the thing which is girded. But on the other hand, *a fissure* is the rift produced by cleaving, not the thing which cleaves it. There seems no reason why *enclosure* may not be used in both senses, that which encloses, and that which is enclosed. We may say of sheep in a fold, "the flock was all within the enclosure," meaning,

within the hurdles surrounding the square; or we may say that "the flock occupied the whole of the enclosure," meaning the whole of the square enclosed. In the case in question, usage seems to have fixed the meaning in the latter of these two senses, viz., the thing enclosed. An envelope is not said to be the enclosure of the letter, but the letter is said to be the enclosure of the envelope. If I write to the Committee of Council on Education, I receive printed directions as to our correspondence, the first of which is, "Every letter *containing enclosures* should enumerate them specially."

115. Clearly however, in strict propriety, the word ought to apply to matter enclosed *in*, and not merely *with*, the letter. But when this is departed from, when we write on a sheet of note-paper, and speak of a drawing three times its size as *the enclosed*, or the *enclosure of this letter*, we may say that we are using the word *letter* in its wider sense, as meaning the envelope as it is received unopened from the post.

116. A curious extension of this license is sometimes found. I remember some years ago receiving a letter from my tailor to the following effect :—" Rev. Sir, *the enclosed* to

your kind order, which hope will give satisfaction, and am, respectfully and obliged." Now "*the enclosed*" in this case was a suit of clothes, sent by coach, and arriving some two days after the letter.

"who" and "which."

117. It will be well to attempt some explanation of the usages of "*who*" and "*which*," especially in our older writers. It may perhaps serve to clear up a matter which may have perplexed some, and to show that there is reason and meaning, where all has appeared confusion and caprice. The common modern distinction between these two forms of the relative pronoun is, that "*who*" is used of persons, "*which*" of things. And this, if borne in mind, will guide us safely throughout. It may be well to notice that what I am about to say does not apply to colloquial English; indeed, hardly to modern English at all : for this reason, that now we do not commonly use either the one or the other of these pronouns, but make the more convenient one, "*that*," do duty for both. We do not say, "the man who met me," nor "the cattle which I saw grazing," but "the man that met me," "the cattle that I saw." We must take care, however, to remember that *which* was not always accounted the neuter of

who, nor is it so in grammar. Dr. Latham says : "To follow the ordinary grammarians, and to call *which* the neuter of *who*, is a blunder. It is no neuter at all, but a compound word." It is made up of *who* and *like:* and this he shows by tracing it through the various Gothic and German forms, till we come to the Scottish *whilk* and the English *which*.

118. Both *who* and *which* are in our older writers used of persons. When this is so, is there any distinction in meaning, and if so, what is it? I think we shall find that the composition of the word *which*, out of *who* and *like*, will in some measure guide us to the answer ; and I think, without presuming to say that every case may be thus explained, that the general account of the two ways is this: "*who*" merely identifies, whereas "*which*" classifies. Let us quote in illustration one of the most important and well-known instances. If, in the solemn address, "Our Father *which* art in heaven," "*who*" had been used instead, then we should have been taught to express only the fact that HE, whom we address as our Father, dwelleth in heaven. But as the sentence now stands, if I understand it rightly, we are taught to express the fact that the relation of Father in which He

stands to us is not an earthly but a heavenly
one ; that whereas there is a fatherhood which
is on earth, His is a Fatherhood which is in
heaven.　And herein I believe that our translators have best followed the mind of Him
who gave us the prayer.　The bare construction of the clause in the original does not
determine for us whether the relative pronoun
applies to the person only of Him whom we
address, or to His title of Father.　But from
our Lord's own use so frequently of the term
"your heavenly Father," I think they were
right in fixing the reference to the relationship,
rather than to the Person only.

Use of
"but."

119. There is a use of the word "*but*,"
principally to be found in our provincial
newspapers, but now and then "leaking up-
wards" into our more permanent literature.
It is when that conjunction is made the con-
necting link between two adjectives which do
not require any such disjoining.　We may
say that a man is *old, but vigorous*, because
vigour united with age is something unexpected ; but we have no right to say *old but
respectable*, because respectability with old age
is not something unexpected.*　Even while I

* The expression "allow me *respectfully, but ear-
nestly* to represent to you," is objected to.　Yet here

write, my train stops at a station on the Great Western Railway, where passengers are invited to take a trip to Glasgow, "to witness the *wild but grand* scenery of Scotland." Now, because scenery is wild, there is no reason why it should not be also grand ; nay, wildness in scenery is most usually an accompaniment of grandeur. *Wild but not grand* would be far more reasonable, because wildness raises an expectation of grandeur, which the "*but*" contradicts.

120. A correspondent writes : " Many, especially I think ladies, say, 'He is not *as* tall as his brother.' Am I not right in saying that after a negative '*so*' should be used—'He is not *so* tall as his brother'?" Such certainly appears to be the usage of our language, however difficult it may be to account for it. We say, "one way of speaking is as good as the other;" but when we deny this proposition, we are obliged to say, "one way of speaking is not so good as the other." *So* cannot be used in the affirmative proposition, nor *as* in the negative. Change the form of

we seem to require the disjunctive particle. A *respectful* representation carries with it the idea of a certain distance and formality, with which the zeal implied in *earnestness* is at first sight inconsistent : and the disjunctive particle seems to show that though the latter is present, the former is not forgotten.

the sentence into one less usual and still allowable, "the one way of speaking is equally good with the other," and the same adverb will serve for both affirmative and negative : "the one is equally good with the other ;" "the one is not equally good with the other."

120*a.* The accuracy of this rule has been called in question by one of my censors, and he gives as his example "There are few artists who draw horses as well as Mr. Leech": in which sentence he rightly observes that "so well" ought to have been used. But why? Simply because the sentence is *not affirmative,* as he designates it, but *negative. There are few* (= not many), *denies* the existence of many : *there are a few, affirms* the existence of some. It never could be said "There are a few artists, who draw horses so well as Mr. Leech." His example confirms the rule, instead of impugning it. Carry the negative a little further, and we have "There are *no* artists who draw horses so well as Mr. Leech."

" had ra-ther."

121. A question has been asked about the expressions "*I had rather,*" "*I had as soon,*" or "*as lief.*" What is the "*had*" in these sentences? Is it really part of the verb

"*have*" at all? If it is, how do we explain it? We cannot use "*to have rather*" in any other tense : it is no recognised phrase in our language. And therefore it has been suggested, that the expression "*I had rather*" has originated with erroneous filling up of the abbreviated *I'd rather*, which is short not for *I had rather*, but *I would rather*. "*I would rather be*" is good English, because "*I would be*" is good English ; but "*I had rather be*" is not good English, because "*I had be*" is not good English.

122. One word with regard to the colloquial contractions which I just now mentioned. We occasionally hear some made use of, which cannot be defended. For instance, "*I ain't certain,*" "*I ain't going.*" This latter, in the past tenses, degenerates still further into the mere vulgarism, "*I warn't going.*" This latter is heard *only* as a vulgarism ; but the other two are very frequently used, even by highly educated persons. The main objection to them is that they are proscribed by usage ; but exception may also be taken to them on their own account. A contraction must surely retain some trace of the resolved form from which it is abbreviated. What, then, is "*ain't?*" It cannot be a contraction of

Colloquial contractions.

"*am not.*"   What "*arn't*" is contracted from
is very plain; it once was "*are not,*" which,
of course, cannot be constructed with the
first person singular.   The only legitimate
colloquial contraction of "*I am not,*" is "*I'm
not:*" "*I'm not going;*" "*I'm not quite sure.*"
The same way of contracting is used in the
case of "*are not.*"   It is usually contracted
by attaching the verb to the personal pronoun, not by combining it with the negative
particle.   We say "*You're not in time,*" not
"*you arn't;*" "*they're not coming,*" not "*they
arn't,*" or "*ain't.*"*

123. A few remarks may be made on the
use in English of feminine substantives.
Certain names of occupations and offices seem
to require them, and others to forbid them.
We say "*emperor*" and "*empress;*" but we
do not in the same sense say "*governor*" and
Feminine
substan-
tives.
"*governess.*"   In this latter case the feminine
form has acquired a meaning of its own, and
refuses to part with it.   I remember, during
the first weeks of our present Queen's reign,

---

* A correspondent complains of the use, by some of
our best writers, of the subjunctive "*thou wert,*" as
equivalent to the indicative "*thou wast.*"   I own I had
not observed it.   Of course there can be no doubt that
it is wrong, wherever it may occur.

hearing a clergyman pray for " *Alexandrina,* our most gracious Queen and *governess.*" Very many, indeed most names of occupations and offices, are common to both sexes, and it savours of pedantry to attempt by adding the feminine termination, to make a difference. The description "*pilgrim,*" for instance, may include both men and women ; yet I saw the other day advertised, " The Wanderings of a *pilgrimess,*" &c. " *Porter* " is another of these words. When we are told to apply to the porter, we are not surprised to see "her that keeps the gate " answer to our knock. But in many public establishments we see the "*portress*" announced as the person to whom we are to apply.* I expect we shall soon see "*groceress* and *tea-dealeress,* and licenced *vendress* of stamps.*" A rule regarding the classification of both sexes together is sometimes forgotten. When both are spoken of under one head, the masculine appellation is used. Thus, though some of the European rulers may be females, they may be correctly classified, when spoken

---

* The *word* " portress " is legitimate enough. We have in Milton " the portress of hell gate." But it does not follow, because it is used in poetry, that we may use it in our common discourse.

of altogether, under the denomination "*kings*."
It has been pointed out that Lord Bacon *
does this even in the case of two, "Ferdi-
nand and Isabella, kings of Spain." This
would hardly be said now; and in ordinary
language, we should perhaps rather choose
to call the European rulers "sovereigns."
But this is no reason why the rule should be
forgotten, nor why sentences, when it is
observed, should be charged with incorrect-
ness, or altered to suit modern ears. A
correspondent writes that his clergyman, in
the following sentence in the prayer for the
Queen, in the Communion service, "We are
taught that the hearts of kings are in Thy
rule and governance," alters the word *kings*
into *sovereigns*.

Punctua-
tion.

124. From speaking of the forms of words,
we will come to punctuation, or stopping. I
remember when I was young in printing, once
correcting the punctuation of a proof-sheet,

---

* A correspondent has charged me with falling into
the blunder of calling this distinguished philosopher
Lord Bacon, which he never was. Surely one who is
contending for usage against pedantry stands acquitted
here. How far the title, "Lord Bacon," has prevailed,
may be seen in the lettering of the backs of the volumes
of the only good edition of his works, that by Heath,
Ellis, and Spedding.

and complaining of the liberties which had been taken with my manuscript. The publisher quietly answered me, that *punctuation was always left to the compositors.* And a precious mess they make of it. The great enemies to understanding anything printed in our language are the *commas.* And these are inserted by the compositors, without the slightest compunction, on every possible occasion. Many words are by rule always hitched off with two commas ; one before and one behind; *nursed,* as the Omnibus Company would call it. *"Too"* is one of these words ; *"however,"* another ; *"also,"* another ; the sense in almost every such case being disturbed, if not destroyed by the process. I remember beginning a sentence with—" However true this may be." When it came in proof, the inevitable comma was after the *"however,"* thus of course making nonsense of my unfortunate sentence. I have some satisfaction in reflecting, that, in the course of editing the Greek text of the New Testament, I believe I have destroyed more than a thousand commas, which prevented the text being properly understood.

125. One very provoking case is that where two adjectives come together, belonging to the same noun-substantive. Thus, in print-

Comma between two adjectives.

ing *a nice young man*, a comma is placed after nice, giving, we may observe, a very different sense from that intended : bringing before us the fact that a man is both nice and young, whereas the original sentence introduced to us a young man that was nice. Thus too in the expression "*a great black dog*," printed without commas, everybody knows what we mean ; but this would be printed " a great, black dog." Take again the case where meaning is intensified by adjectives being repeated—as in "*the wide wide world*," "*the deep deep sea.*" Such expressions you almost invariably find printed "*the wide, wide world*," "*the deep, deep sea*," thereby making them, if judged by any rule at all, absolute nonsense.

Too few commas.

126. Still, though too many commas are bad, too few are not without inconvenience also. I saw the other day a notice of " the Society for Promoting the Observance of the Lord's-day which was founded in 1831," giving the notion that the *day, not the society*, was founded in that year. Had the date been 1631, instead of 18, an awkward interpretation might have been possible.

127. I take the following, verbatim and *punctuatim*, from a religious newspaper of

this present year : "EDUCATION. — In a Ladies' School conducted on Evangelical principles about nine in number, good instruction is given, &c."

128. While I am upon stops, a word is necessary concerning notes of admiration. A note of admiration consists, as we know, of a point with an upright line suspended over it, strongly suggestive of a gentleman jumping off the ground with amazement. These *shrieks,* as they have been called, are scattered up and down the page by the compositors without mercy. If one has written the words "*O sir,*" as they ought to be written, and are written in Genesis xliii. 20, viz., with the plain capital "O" and no stop, and then a comma after "*Sir,*" our friend the compositor is sure to write "*Oh*" with a shriek (!) and to put another shriek after "*Sir.*" Use, in writing, as few as possible of these nuisances. They always make the sense weaker, where you can possibly do without them. The only case I know of where they are really necessary, is where the language is pure exclamation, as in "How beautiful is night ! " or, "O that I might find him ! "

Notes of admiration.

129. The very simple and intelligible word "*centre*" comes in for a good deal of mal-

"centre.

treatment in our days. *Centre* is from the Greek word *"Kentron,"* meaning merely *a point :* the point of a needle, or of a sting, or of anything else : and hence is used in geometry to denote that point round which a circle or any other symmetrical curve is drawn. And in accordance with this its original meaning ought its use always to be : a centre should always designate a point, never a line, nor, except as presently defined, a middle space. But we see this often departed from. "A gangway will be left down the centre of the room," is a clear case of such departure. I do not of course mean to advocate absolute strictness in this or in any other usage. Accuracy is one thing, punctiliousness is another. The one should be always observed, the other always avoided. While I should take care not to say that I *walked up and down the centre* of the lawn, I should not object to say that there is a large bed of geraniums *in the centre*, although strictly speaking the centre of the lawn is in the bed, not the bed in the centre.*

---

* A correspondent informs me, that a parliamentary notice to landowners, which has been in use for the last seventeen years, and is issued to the number of hundreds of thousands at once, contains the words "within

130. And in the figurative use of this word, and of all words, intelligent common sense, rather than punctiliousness, ought to be our guide. *Centre*, and its adjective *central*, are often used in speaking of objects of thought, as well as of sight. Let it be borne in mind, when this is done, that these words apply only to a principal object round which others group themselves, and not to one which happens to be pre-eminent amongst others. To say that some conspicuous person in an assembly was *the centre of attraction*, is perfectly correct ; but to say that some subject of conversation, merely because it happened to occupy more of the time than other subjects, was the *central topic* of the evening, is incorrect and unmeaning.

131. Ought we to write *by and by*, or *by and bye ? by the by*, or *by the bye ?* There is a tendency to add a vowel, by way of giving emphasis in pronunciation, when a preposition is used as an adverb. Thus " *too* " is only the preposition " *to*," emphasized ; a " *bye* "

"by and by."

---

eleven yards, or thereabouts, of the *centre-line* of the proposed work." This is not absolutely wrong : for the *centre-line* is the line which *passes through the centre*, as the *Chatham-line* is the line which passes through Chatham.

ball, at cricket, is only a ball that runs *by*. In this latter case the added "*e*" is universal: but not so in *by-play*, *by-end*, which are sometimes spelt with it and sometimes without it. And we never add it when "*by*" is used as an adverb in construction in a sentence, as in *passing by*. This being so, it is better, perhaps, to confine this way of spelling to the only case where it seems needed, the *bye ball*, and to write "*by and by*," "*by the by*."

"endeavour
ourselves." 132. A mistake is very generally made by our clergy in reading the collect for the second Sunday after Easter. We there pray, with reference to Our Lord's death for us, and His holy example, "that we may thankfully receive that his inestimable benefit, and also daily endeavour ourselves to follow the blessed steps of his most holy life." This is often read with an emphasis on the word "*ourselves*," as if it were in the nominative case, and to be distinguished from some other person. But no other persons have been mentioned ; and the sense thus becomes confused for the hearer. The fact is, that "*ourselves*" is not in the nominative case at all, but in the accusative after the verb "*endeavour*," which at the time of the compiling of our

Prayer-book was used as a reflective verb. To *endeavour myself*, is to consider myself in duty bound. That this is so, appears clearly from the answer given in the Ordination service, where the Bishop asks, "Will you be diligent in prayers and in reading of the Holy Scriptures, and in such studies as help to the knowledge of the same . . . ?" And the candidate replies, "I will *endeavour myself* so to do, the Lord being my helper."

133. The usage of the verb to *mistake* is somewhat anomalous. Its etymology seems simple enough—*to take amiss*. And by the analogy of "misunderstand," "misinterpret," "mislead," "misinform," "miscalculate," it ought to be simply an active verb, as in the phrases, "you mistook my meaning," "he had mistaken the way." This would give as its passive use, "my meaning was mistaken by you." But our English usage is different; we have these phrases, it is true, but we far more commonly use the verb in the passive, to carry what should be its active meaning. To *be mistaken* is not, with us, to be misapprehended by another, but to commit a mistake oneself. This is a curious translation of meaning, but it is now rooted in the

"to be mistaken."

language and become idiomatic. "I thought so, but I was mistaken," is universally said, not "I mistook." We expect to hear "you are mistaken," and should be surprised at hearing asserted "you are mistaking," or "you mistake," unless followed by an accusative, "the meaning," or "me." When we hear the former of these, we begin to consider whether we were right or wrong; when the latter, we at once take the measure of our friend, as one who has not long escaped from the study of the rules of the lesser grammarians, by which, and not by the usages of society, circumstances have compelled him to learn his language.

"good looking" or "well looking." 134. A correspondent asks me, *good looking* or *well looking?* Here is another instance of idiom versus accuracy. And idiom decidedly has it. To speak of a *well-looking* man would be to make oneself ridiculous: all usage is against the word. But, at the same time, to be *good looking* is not to *look good.* It is, in one sense, to *look well;* or, if we will, to have good looks. So that the whole matter seems to be left to usage, which in this case is decisive.

"latter," of more than two; "last," of only two. 135. One point made very much of by the precisians is, the avoiding of the use of "*latter*" when we have spoken of more than two things, and of "*last*" when we have spoken of only two. Is this founded in any necessity or propriety of the laws of thought ; or is it a mere arbitrary regulation laid down by persons who know little and care little about those laws?

136. Let us inquire into the matter. The notion is, that in speaking of two things, we can have only positive and comparative; that for a superlative we require three or more ; and when we have three or more, we must use the superlative. Thus if I speak of two invasions of Great Britain, I must call the earlier the *former*, not the *first*, and the second the *latter*, not the *last*. But if I speak of three invasions, I must call the third, in referring to it, the *last*, not the *latter*. Is there reason in this? Let us look at it in this light. Of two invasions, the earlier is undoubtedly the *first*, the later the *second*. Now "*first*" is a superlative ; and if of two, one is designated by a superlative, why not the other?

137. Still, this is not digging to the root of the matter ; it is only arguing from the acknowledged use of a form in one case, to its legitimate use in an analogous one. Let us take it in another point of view. "*First*"

is unavoidably used of that one in a series with which we begin, whatever be the number which follow; whether many or few. Why should not "*last*" be used of that one in a series with which we end, whatever be the number which preceded, whether many or few? The second invasion, when we spoke of only two, was undoubtedly the *last* mentioned; and surely therefore may be spoken of in referring back to it, as the last, without any violation of the laws of thought.

138. Nor does the comparative of necessity suggest that only two are concerned, though it may be more *natural* to speak of the *greatest* of more than two, not of the *greater.* For that which is *greatest* of any number, is *greater* than the rest.

"superior," "inferior."

139. There is an expression creeping into general use which cannot be justified in grammar, "a *superior* man;" "a very *inferior* person." We all know what is meant: and a certain sort of defence may be set up for it by calling it elliptical: by saying that the comparatives are to be filled up by inserting "to most men," or the like. But with all its convenience, and all the defence which can be set up for it, this way of speaking is not desirable; and if followed out as a precedent,

cannot but vulgarize and deteriorate our
language.

140. We seem rather unfortunate in our "talented."
designations for our men of ability. For
another term by which we describe them,
"*talented*," is about as bad as possible. What
is it? It looks like a participle. From what
verb? Fancy such a verb as "*to talent!*"
Coleridge somewhere cries out against this
newspaper word, and says, Imagine other participles formed by this analogy, and men being
said to be pennied, shillinged, or pounded.
He perhaps forgot that, by an equal abuse,
men are said to be "*moneyed*" men, or as
we sometimes see it spelt (as if the word itself
were not bad enough without making it
worse by false orthography), "*monied*."

141. Another formation of this kind, "gifted."
"*gifted*," is at present very much in vogue.
Every man whose parts are to be praised, is
a *gifted* author, or speaker, or preacher. Nay,
sometimes a very odd transfer is made, and
the pen with which the author writes is said
to be "*gifted*," instead of himself.

142. Exception has been taken to what has "to leave,"
been called the *neuter* use of the verb to absolute.
leave: "I shall not *leave* before December 1."
But it is not correct to describe this as a

neuter use; it is rather the *absolute* use.
The verb is still active, but the object is
suppressed. Thus, if there are three persons
in a room, one reading the Bible, another the
newspaper, and the third a review, I say
that they are all *reading*, without depriving
the verb of its active force; using it as an
absolute predicate applicable to them all. Thus
too, if of three persons one is leaving his own
home to-morrow, another a friend's house, and
the third an hotel, I may say that they are all
leaving to-morrow. And this absolute usage
is perfectly legitimate where one person only
is concerned. " I shall not read this morning,
but I shall write." "It is my intention to
leave when my lease is up." How far it
may be more or less elegant under given circumstances to speak thus, is another question,
which can only be decided when those circumstances are known; but of the correctness of
the usage I imagine there can be no doubt.

" could not
got."

143. Connected with the last are, or may
seem to be, certain elliptical usages which cannot be similarly defended. Thus when the
object has been to visit a friend, or to attain
a certain point, we sometimes hear the excuse
for failure thus expressed, " I meant to come
to you,"—or, " I fully intended to be there;"

"but *I couldn't get.*" The full expression would in this case be, " I couldn't get to you;" or, "I couldn't get there." But the verb "*to get*" is used in so many meanings, that it is hardly fit for this elliptical position. Besides that the sentence ends inelegantly and inharmoniously, an ambiguity is suggested: "couldn't get what?" a horse? or time? or money to pay the fare? or some one to show the way?

144. Another word objectionably thus used is the verb "*to belong.*" "Is Miss A. coming to the Amateur Concert to-night?" "No: she does not *belong;*" meaning, does not belong to the Society. And then perhaps we are told that "though she does not *belong* this year, she means to *belong* next." Here again we may say that *belong* is a verb of so wide a signification, that it will hardly admit of being thus detached from its accidents, and used absolutely and generally. *"does not belong."*

144*a*. I am reminded by a valued correspondent, of another use of the verb " *to belong,*" already familiar to me, as having been long resident in the north-midland counties. " We have," he says, "in these parts a provincial usage of the word "*belong:*" as, "belong to Halifax," " belong to Leeds :" or, more com- *to "belong Leeds," &c.*

monly, "belong Halifax," "belong Leeds:"
meaning, live there. The late Mr. F. W., one
of the largest proprietors of land in York-
shire, and M.P. for the yet undivided county
—and, let me add, a wise and munificent
friend to the Church,—was withal so little
lavish on his person, that he might easily pass
for a very humble farmer. He was one day
accosted on the roadside by two strangers in
a gig on their way to Wighill, near York.
"My man, do you belong Wighill?" He
answered, "No, Sirs, Wighill belongs to me."

"to pro-
gress."

145. The verb to "*progress*," is challenged
by one of my friends as a modern Ameri-
canism. This is not strictly accurate. Shakspeare uses it in King John, act v. sc. 2 :

> "Let me wipe off this honourable dew,
>   That silverly doth *progress* on thy cheeks." *

But you will observe that the line requires
the verb to be pronounced prógress, not pro-

---

* I mention, as in courtesy bound, an account of this
construction which has been sent me by a correspondent
anxious to vindicate Shakspeare from having used a
modern vulgarism. He would understand "doth progress" as "doeth progress," the latter word being a
substantive. Surely, he can hardly be in earnest. [I am
surprised to see this advocated in the very sensible little
English Grammar of Mr. Higginson.   Aug. 1864.]

gréss, so that this is perhaps hardly a case in point, except as to the word, a verb formed on the noun *progress*.

146. Milton also uses such a verb, in the magnificent peroration of his "Treatise of Reformation in England." I cannot forbear citing the whole passage, as it may be a relief to my readers and to myself in the midst of these verbal enquiries :

Passage from Milton.

"Then amidst the Hymns and Hallelujahs of saints, some one may perhaps be heard offering at high strains in new and lofty measures, to sing and celebrate thy divine mercies, and marvellous judgments in this land throughout all ages ; whereby this great and warlike nation, instructed and inured to the fervent and continual practice of Truth and Righteousness, and casting far from her the rags of her old vices, may press on hard to that high and happy Emulation, to be found the soberest, wisest, and most Christian people at that day, when Thou the Eternal and shortly expected King, shalt open the clouds to judge the several kingdoms of the world, and distributing national honours and rewards to religious and just commonwealths, shalt put an end to all earthly Tyrannies, proclaiming thy universal and mild Monarchy through heaven and earth.   Where they undoubtedly, that by their labours, counsels and prayers, have been earnest for the common good of Religion and their country, shall receive above the inferior orders of the Blessed, the regal addition of Principalities, Legions, and Thrones into their glorious Titles, and, in supereminence of beatifick vision, *progressing* the dateless and irrevoluble circle of Eternity, shall clasp inseparable Hands with Joy and Bliss, in over measure for ever."

147. It may be noticed again that Milton's use of the verb is not exactly that which is become common now.   He seems to make it equivalent to "*moving along,*" or "*moving throughout,*" in an active sense.   These favoured ones are to *progress* the circle of Eternity, *i.e.*, I suppose, to revolve for ever round and round it.   The present usage makes the verb neuter ; to *progress* meaning to advance, to make progress.   I can hardly say I feel much indignation against the word, thus used. We seem to want it ; and if we do, and it does not violate any known law of formation, by all means let us have it.   True, it is the first of its own family; we have not yet formed *aggress*, *regress*, *egress*, or *retrogress*,*

* One of my Censors has found some of these words

into verbs ; but we have done in substance
the same thing, by having admitted long ago
the verbs *suggest, digest, project, object, reject,
eject;* for all these are formed from the same
part of the original Latin verbs, as this "*progress*" on which we have been speaking.

148. In treating of this verb to "*progress,*" Nouns made into verbs.
a correspondent notices that there prevails a
tendency to turn nouns into verbs : "The
ship remained to *coal:*" "the church is being
pewed:" "he was prevailed on to *head* the
movement." I do not see that we can object
to this tendency in general, seeing that it has
grown with the growth of our language, and
under due regulation is one of the most
obvious means of enriching it. Verbs thus
formed will carry themselves into use, in spite
of the protests of the purists. Some years

set down as English verbs in the folio edition of Bailey's
Universal Dictionary, published in 1755. But there
is as wide a difference between *dictionary words* and
English words, as between vocabulary French and
spoken French. We might in a few minutes find a
list of dictionary words which would introduce us to
some strange acquaintances. What do we think of
"abarcy," "aberuncate," "abolishable," "abstringe,"
"abstrude," "acervate," "acetosity," "adjugate,"
"admetiate," "adminicle," "advolation," "adus-
tible," &c., &c. Thousands of words in the Dictionaries are simply Latin, made English in form, without
any authority for their use.

ago, precise scholars used to exclaim against the verb "*to experience;*" and a very ugly candidate for admission into the language it was. Milton introduced its participle when he wrote, "He through the arméd files Darts his *experienced* eye." Still, as we know in the case of "*talented*" and "*moneyed*," the participle may be tolerated long before the verb is invented: and no instance of the verb "*to experience*" occurs till quite recently. But all attempts to exclude it *now* would be quite ineffectual.*

"to treat of," or "to treat?"

149. To *treat of*, or *to treat?* Plainly, which we please. To *treat* is to *handle*, to *have under treatment*, to *discuss*. The verb may be used with an object following it, to

---

* A correspondent referred to me the question whether in Milton's line,

"Then let the pealing organ blow,"

the verb "*blow*" is rightly used. The organ, it was urged, *is blown:* and it might as well be said that the fire "*blows*," when it is blown.

But I believe Milton to be quite correct. The whole action of the organ is, to produce sound by *blowing* into the pipes : and this it is, rather than the filling the bellows with wind, that is meant. The action of fire is, not to blow, but to burn : when it *is blown*, it *burns:* but when the organ *is blown*, it, by aid of its valves, opened by the pressure on the keys, *blows*, and produces music.

"*treat a subject :*" or it may be used absolutely, to "*treat concerning,*" or "*of,*" a subject. It is one of those very many cases so little understood by the layers down of precise rules, where writers and speakers are left to choose, as the humour takes them, between different ways of expression.

149*a*. And I may once for all notice a fallacious way of arguing, into which the sciolists who would legislate for our language are continually betrayed. It consists in assuming that, of two modes of expression, if one be shown to be right, the other must necessarily be wrong. Whereas very often the varying expressions are equally legitimate, and each of them full of interest, as bearing traces of the different sources from which our language has sprung.

Fallacy :—of two ways of expression, one must be wrong.

150. There is a piece of affectation becoming sadly common among our younger clergy, which I had already marked for notice, when I received a letter, from which the following is an extract :—"I wish to call your attention to the ignorance which is sometimes exhibited by clergy and others of the true meaning of the preposition in such expressions as 'the city of Canterbury,' 'the play of "Hamlet."'" We sometimes hear it pro-

" the book Genesis," " the city London."

claimed from the desk, 'Here beginneth the first chapter of the book Genesis:' and we read in parochial documents of 'the parish of St. George,' 'the parish of St. Mary,' instead 'of St. George's,' 'of St. Mary's,' &c."

151. I believe the excuse, if it can be called one, set up for this violation of usage is, that "the book of Genesis" and "the book of Daniel" cannot both be right, because the former was not written by Genesis, as the latter was by Daniel. But, as my correspondent says, this simply betrays ignorance of the meanings of the preposition "*of*." It is used, in designations of this kind, in three different senses: 1. To denote authorship, as "*the book of Daniel:*" 2. To denote subject-matter, as "*the first book of Kings:*" 3. As a note of apposition, signifying, "which is," or "which is called," as "*the book of Genesis,*" "*of Exodus,*" &c. This last usage meets us at every turn; and the pedant who ignores it in the reading desk, must, in consistency, drop it everywhere else. Imagine his letter describing his summer holiday: "I left the city London, and passed through the county Kent, leaving the realm England at the town Dover, and entering the empire France at the

town Calais, on my way to the Republic Switzerland." *

152. I may remark in passing, that here again usage comes in with its prescriptive laws, and prevents the universal application of rules. While we always say "the city of Cairo," not "the city Cairo," we never say "the river of Nile," but always "the river Nile." So too "the city of London," but "the river Thames."

153. It seems astonishing that many of our writers should not yet be clear in their distinctive use of "rever*end*" and "rever*ent*." I saw lately a description of a certain person as being "unintentionally irreverend." The writer (or printer) of this forgot that *"reverent"* (*reverens,-entis*) is the *subjĕctive* word, describing the feeling within a man as its subject, whereas *"reverend"* (*reverendus*) is the *objective* word, describing the feeling with which a man is regarded,—of which he is the object from without. Dean Swift might be "very reverend," by common courtesy ; but he was certainly not "very reverent" in his conduct or in his writings.

" reverend,"
and " re-
verent."

154. A few words more about these *subjective* and *objective* words. It has been the fashion

Subjective
and objec-
tive words

* See note E, at the end of the volume.

to laugh at and decry these terms, *subjective* and *objective.* I have generally found that those who do so are wanting in appreciation of the distinction which these words are intended to convey, and which can hardly be conveyed but by their use. Take the case where one and the same word is used in both senses. We say "a fearful heart," and we say "a fearful height." In the former phrase we use *fearful* in its *subjective* sense, as describing a quality inherent in the subject of the sentence; in the latter phrase, we use *fearful* in its *objective* sense, as describing an effect produced on those who are the objects contemplated. How otherwise than by the use of these terms are we clearly and shortly to indicate this difference? Other instances of this double use of one and the same word may be found in "a hopeful spirit," "a hopeful youth," —"a joyful multitude," "a joyful occasion;" and an example of the distinction in the use of two words, in the adjectives "*tall*" (subjective,—high with reference to himself as compared with others) and "*high*" (objective, contemplated as an object from without).

"or" and "nor" in a negative sentence.

155. A good deal of confusion is prevalent in the usages of "*or*" and "*nor*" in

a negative sentence. When I wrote, in the last paragraph but one, "he was certainly not very reverent in his conduct or in his writings," was I right or wrong? Ought I to have said, "he was not very reverent in his conduct *nor* in his writings?" We may regard this sentence in two ways, which may be represented by the two following modes of punctuation : 1. "He was not very reverent in his conduct, or in his writings." 2. "He was not very reverent, in his conduct or in his writings." According to the former punctuation, "*or*" is wrong; it should be "*nor*." But observe that thus we get a somewhat awkward elliptical sentence : "He was not very reverent in his conduct, nor (was he very reverent) in his writings." In the second form of the sentence, "*or*" is right, and "*nor*" would be wrong. This will be evident in a moment by filling up the sentence with the other alternative particle, "He was not very reverent, *either* in his conduct *or* in his writings ;" not, "He was not very reverent, *neither* in his conduct, *nor* in his writings."

156. We may, if we will, strike out the negative altogether from the part of the sentence containing the verb, and attach it entirely to the alternative clauses. But in

this case it is usual to place those clauses before the predicative portion of the sentence: "neither in his conduct, nor in his writings was he very reverent."

Elliptical sentences.

157. As I have been speaking of an elliptical sentence, I may remark that it is astonishing what an amount of ellipsis the English ear will tolerate: in other words, how great an effort the mind of a hearer will make in supplying that which is suppressed. This extends sometimes even to changing the construction, and turning affirmative into negative, tacitly and unconsciously, as the sentence falls upon the eye or ear. A remarkable example of this occurs in one of the most solemn prayers in our English Communion Service: "We do not presume to come to this Thy Table, most merciful Lord, trusting in our own righteousness; but (*we do presume to come, trusting*) in thy manifold and great mercies." Put this admirable sentence into the hands of our ordinary rhetoricians, and it would be utterly marred. The apparently awkward ellipsis would be removed thus: "We presume to come to this Thy Table, trusting, not in our own righteousness, but in thy manifold and great mercies." But at the same time, the whole character of the sentence

and of the prayer would be altered. Who does not see, that by the opening words, "We do not presume," the *key-note* of the whole prayer is struck—the disclaiming of presumption founded on our own righteousness? It was worth any subsequent halting of the sentence in mere accuracy of construction, to secure this plain declaration of the spirit in which the prayer was about to be made.

158. And this leads us to a rule which we should do well to follow in all such cases. To secure the right sense being given, and the right emphasis laid, is the first thing : not to satisfy the rules of the rhetoricians. Many a sentence, which the mere rhetorician would pronounce faulty in arrangement, does its work admirably, and has done it for centuries : let him correct it and re-arrange it, and it will do that work no more. Its strong emphasis will have disappeared : its nervous homeliness will have departed, and it will sink down into vapid commonplace.

General rule in such cases.

159. Let us now enter on this matter somewhat more in detail. The one rule which is supposed by the ordinary rhetoricians to regulate the arrangement of words in sentences, is this : that "*those parts of a sentence which are most closely connected in their meaning, should*

Arrangement of words in sentences.

be as closely as possible connected in position;"
or, as it is propounded by Dr. Blair, *"A
capital rule in the arrangement of sentences is
that the words or members most nearly related
should be placed in the sentence as near to each
other as possible, so as to make their mutual
relation clearly appear."*

Ordinary
ule.

160. Now doubtless this rule is, in the
main, and for general guidance, a good and
useful one: indeed, so plain to all, that it
surely needed no inculcating.   But there are
more things in the English language than
seem to have been dreamt of in the philosophy of the rhetoricians. If this rule were uniformly applied, it would break down the force
and the living interest of style in any English
writer, and reduce his matter, as we just now
said, to a dreary and dull monotony.   For it
is in exceptions to its application, that almost
all vigour and character of style consist.   Of
this I shall give abundant illustration by-and-
by.   Meantime let me make some remarks
on two very important matters in the construction of sentences: the requirements of
emphasis, and the requirements of *parenthesis;*
neither of which are taken into account by
the ordinary rule.

Emphasis.

161. Emphasis means the stress, or force of

intonation, which the intended sense requires *requires its violation,* to be laid on certain words, or changes, in a sentence. Very often (not always) we can indicate this by the form and arrangement of the sentence itself. Some languages have far greater capacities this way than our own; but we are able commonly to do it sufficiently for the careful and intelligent reader.

162. Now how is this done? A sentence arranged according to the rule above cited, simply conveys the meaning of its words in their ordinary and straightforward construction; and in English, owing to the difficulty, often felt, of departing from this arrangement, we must very generally be contented with it, at the risk of our words not conveying the fullness of the meaning which we intended. For let me explain, that whenever we wish to indicate that a stress is to be laid on a certain word, or clause, in a sentence, we must do it by taking that word or that clause out of its natural place which it would hold by the above rule, and putting it into some more prominent one. A substantive, for example, governed by a verb, is in a subordinate position to that verb; the mind of the reader is arrested by the verb, rather than by the substantive; so that if for any rea-

son we wish to make the substantive prominent, we must provide some other place
for it than next to the verb which governs
it.

In the case
of words;

163. Take, as an example, the words *"he
restored me to mine office:"* where the words are
arranged in accordance with the ordinary law,
and the idea expressed is the simple one of
restoration to office. But suppose a distinction
is to be made between the narrator, who had
been restored to office, and another man, who
had been very differently treated. Of course
we might still observe the rule, and say " He
restored me to mine office, and he hanged
him;" but the sentence becomes thus (and it
is to this that I request the reader's attention)
a very tame one, not expressing the distinction
in itself, nor admitting of being so read as to
express it sharply and decisively. Now, let
us violate the rule, and see how the sentence
reads: *" Me he restored unto mine office, and
him he hanged."* Thus wrote our translators
of Genesis (xli. 13), and they arranged the
words rightly. No reader, be his intelligence
ever so little, can help reading this sentence
as it ought to be read.

164. And let there be no mistake about
this being a violation of the rule. The words

nearest connected are "*restored*," and "*me*," which it governs: "*hanged*," and "*him*," which it governs. When I take "*me*" out of its place next "*restored*," and begin the sentence with it, letting the pronoun "*he*" come between them, I do most distinctly violate the rule, that those words which are most nearly connected in the sense should also be most nearly connected in the arrangement. I have purposely chosen this first instance of the simplest possible kind, to make the matter clear as we advance into it. Let us take another. St. Peter (Acts ii. 23) says to the Jews, speaking of our Lord, "Him, being delivered by the determinate counsel and foreknowledge of God, ye have taken, and by wicked hands have crucified and slain." Here we have the pronoun "*Him*" placed first in the sentence, and at a considerable distance from the verbs that govern it, with the clause, "being delivered by the determinate counsel and foreknowledge of God," inserted between. Yet, who does not see that the whole force of that which was intended to be conveyed by the sentence is thus gained, and could not otherwise be gained? Arranged according to the common rule, the sentence would have been, "Ye have taken Him, being delivered by the determinate counsel and foreknowledge of God, and by wicked hands have crucified and slain Him;" and the whole force and point would have been lost.

and paren-
thesis, in
the case of
clauses.

165. And as this necessity for bringing into prominence affects the position of words in sentences, so does it also that of clauses. A clause is often subordinate in the construction to some word or some other clause; while it is the object of the writer to bring the subordinate, not the principal, clause into prominence. And then, as we saw with regard to words just now, the clause which is inferior in constructive importance is brought out and transposed, so that the reader's attention may be arrested by it. Or perhaps the writer feels the necessity of noticing as he passes on, certain particulars which will come in flatly, and spoil the balance of the sentence, if reserved till their proper place. Such passing notices are called "*parentheses,*" from a Greek word, meaning *insertion by the way;* and every such insertion is a violation of the supposed universal rule of position.

166. Thus, for example, I am narrating a circumstance which, when it happened, excited my astonishment. Undoubtedly the natural order of constructing the sentence

would be to relate what happened first, and my surprise at it afterwards. "I was looking at a man walking on the bank of the river, when he suddenly turned about, and plunged in, to my great surprise." But who does not see the miserable way in which the last clause drags behind, and loses all force? We therefore take this clause out of its place, and insert it before that to which it applies, and with which it ought to be constructed: we word the sentence thus: "I was looking at a man walking on the bank of the river, when, to my great surprise, he suddenly turned round, and plunged in." I need not further illustrate so common a transposition: I will only say that it produces instances of violation of the supposed rule of arrangement in almost every extant page of good English; and in common conversation, every day, and all day long.

167. Sometimes these insertions are such obvious interruptions to the construction, that they are marked off by brackets, and it is thus made evident that the sentence is intended to flow on as if they did not exist; but far more frequently they are without any such marks, and the common sense of the reader is left to separate them off for himself.

It is impossible to write lucidly or elegantly
without the use of these parenthetical clauses.
Care ought of course to be taken that they
be not so inserted as to mislead the reader
by introducing the possibility of constructing
the sentence otherwise than as the writer
intended.   But at the same time it may be
fearlessly stated, that not one of our best
writers has ever been minutely scrupulous on
this point : and that there does not exist in
our language one great work in prose or in
poetry, in which may not be found numerous
instances of possible misconstruction arising
from this cause.   And this has not been from
carelessness, but because the writer was
intent on expressing his meaning in good
manly English, and was not anxious as to
the faults which carping and captious critics
might find with his style.   Lord Kames gives
a rule that "*a circumstance ought never to be
placed between two capital members of a sentence : or if so placed* (I suppose he means, *if
it be so placed*), *the first word in the consequent
member should be one that cannot connect it
with what precedes.*"

168. Any one on the look out for misun-
derstanding may convince himself by trial,
that there is hardly a page in any English

book which will not furnish him with instances
of violation of this rule.

169. Let my examples begin at home. One
of my censors quoted as faulty in this respect
the following sentence, which occurred in these
notes : I said that certain persons "fall, from
their ignorance, into absurd mistakes." The
parenthetical clause here is "from their ignorance." My censor would amend it thus—
"certain persons, in consequence of their ignorance, fall into absurd mistakes." Now this
is not what I wanted to say ; at least it is a
blundering and roundabout way of expressing
it. The purpose is, to bring the fact stated
into prominence: and this is done by making
the verb "*fall*" immediately follow its subject, "*certain persons.*" According to the
proposed arrangement, it is the fact of what is
about to be stated being a consequence of
their ignorance, which is put into the place of
prominence and emphasis. Very well, then :
having stated that they *fall*, and being about
to say *into what*, it is convenient, in order to
keep the sentence from dragging a comparatively unimportant clause at its end, to bring
in that clause, containing the reason of the
fall, immediately after the verb itself. To
my mind, the clause, in spite of the

possible ambiguity, reads far better with "*from*" than with "*in consequence of*," which is too heavy and lumbering. The "*possibility of a ludicrous interpretation*" which my censor speaks of—the *falling from ignorance* as a man falls from grace, or falls from virtue, seems to me to be effectually precluded in the mind of any man who happens to remember that ignorance is neither a grace nor a virtue. Really, we do not write for idiots: and it must require, to speak in the genteel language which some of my correspondents uphold, a most abnormal elongation of the auricular appendages, for a reader to have suggested to his mind a fall from the sublime height of ignorance down into the depth of a mistake.

170. There are one or two more expressions of mine which have been found fault with, well worth noticing for the illustrations which they will furnish on matters connected with our present subject. There has been quoted with disapprobation a sentence of mine in paragraph 2 of these notes, which originally stood thus: "Would have been broken to pieces in a deep rut, or come to grief in a bottomless swamp." It is said that this can only be filled in thus, "Would have

been broken to pieces, ... or would have been come to grief in a bottomless swamp:" "for," it is added, "a part of a complex tense means nothing without the rest of the tense." That is, I suppose, the whole of the auxiliary verbs which belong to the first verb in a sentence must also belong to all other verbs which are coupled to that first verb. Now, is this so? I do not find that our best writers observe any such rule. In Deut. vi. 11, Israel is admonished, *"When thou shalt have eaten and be full, beware lest thou forget the Lord."* We all know that this means: "When thou shalt have eaten and shalt be full." But, according to my censor, it must be filled up, "When thou shalt have eaten and shalt have be full."

171. You might, by applying to any chapter in the Bible the same treatment of which I have just been giving examples, show it to be full of ambiguities, which no one in all these generations has ever found out. Take examples from one chapter, Acts xxii. In verse 4, I read, *"And I persecuted this way unto the death."* This violates the supposed law of arrangement, and falls under the charge of ambiguity. The gospel might, according to these critics, be understood from it to be a

From Scripture.

way unto death instead of a way unto life.
Take again verse 29, "*Then they departed from
him which should have examined him.*" Now
we all know what this means. It is a more
neat way of expressing what would be the
regularly arranged sentence, "*Then they which
should have examined him departed from him.*"
But here again the captious and childish critic
may find ambiguity—"Then they departed—
from him which should have examined him."

Grammar
of our au-
thorised
version :

I must not, however, forget that some of my
correspondents find it convenient to depreciate
the language and grammar of our authorised
version of Scripture.* I would recommend

---

* One gentleman says : "When I was at school, it
was the habit of my tutor to give his class specimens of
bad English for correction. You will be surprised to
hear, that those specimens were chiefly texts from
Scripture. They were given with all reverence, never-
theless. It was because the readiest examples were to
be had from the Bible, that any were taken from that
source at all. Again, Shakspeare is held up by you as
a pattern to modern grammarians. With all respect, I
cannot understand how any man, with the education
that you must have received, could venture even to
insinuate such a dogma as this. Any one, with even
the insufficient light which Murray affords, may detect
numberless errors in every play which Shakspeare has
written." This is rich indeed. One can well conceive
the sort of English which was taught at my correspondent's school. And very much of the degenerate Eng-

them to try the experiment of amending that language. They may then perhaps find that what the translators themselves once said is true. A story is told, that they had a recommendation from a correspondent to alter a certain word in their version, giving *five* sufficient reasons for the change. They are said to have replied that they had already considered the matter, and had *fifteen* sufficient reasons *against* the change. I think if my correspondents can bring themselves to consider reasonably any passage in which the English grammar of our authorised version appears doubtful, they will find themselves in the same predicament as this correspondent of the translators. I have often tried the experiment, and this has generally been the result. Mind, our present question is not that of their having adequately translated the Greek, but whether or not they wrote their own language grammatically and clearly.

172. Still, lest I should seem to be a "man of one book only," I will give from our greatest English writer, an instance (from among many) of what would be called

of Shakspeare.

lish of our day is to be traced to such instruction. I should like to have seen some of the tutor's corrected texts.

a similar ambiguity. In the "Two Gentle-men of Verona," act. i. scene 2, Julia says:—

> " O hateful hands, to tear such loving words !
> Injurious wasps, to feed on such sweet honey,
> And kill the bees that yield it with your stings."

According to my correspondents, we ought to understand this as saying that the bees yield the honey by means of the wasps' stings.

Best way of proceeding in regard of such rules.

173. But I conceive we have had enough of these so-called universal rules. All I would say on them to my younger readers is, the less you know of them, the less you turn your words right or left to observe them, the better. Write good manly English; explain what you mean, as sensible intelligent men cannot fail to understand it, and then, if the rules be good, you will be sure to have complied with them; and if they be bad, your writing will be a protest against them. See the " Edinburgh Review," quoted in note on paragraph 189.

Real ambiguity.

174. It is not difficult to distinguish the sentences whose arrangement I have been defending, from those in which real ambiguity arises. Take the following as examples. I found it in one of the daily papers :—"The most interesting news from Italy is that of

the trial of the thieves who robbed the bank
of Messrs. Parodi at Genoa, on May 1, 1862,
in open daylight, which commenced at Genoa
on the 5th." In a letter addressed to another
paper, this sentence occurs: "I with my family
reside in the parish of Stockton, which consists
of my wife and daughters."

175. Now both these sentences are instructive to us. We may see from them how such
ambiguity really arises: viz., by the occurrence,
between the antecedent and its pronoun, of
another word, which naturally suggests to the
mind of the hearer a connection with the following pronoun. In both these sentences this
is the case. Daylight is said to commence at
a certain time, as well as a trial: a parish is
said to consist of certain persons, as well as
a family. Hence the ambiguity: and not,
as is often maintained, from the mere form
of the sentence. Any one so disposed may
cull sentences out of any English writer,
not even excepting Lord Macaulay, and
show that they *may* be understood in a
certain number of hundred, or thousand, different ways. But the simple answer is, that
nobody ever *will* so understand them: and,
as has been seen, there are often reasons why
the apparently ambiguous form should be

preferred to the strictly perspicuous one, as being more forcible, putting the emphatic word or clause in the proper place, or even as avoiding stiffness and awkwardness of sound. Let your style be idiomatic, simple, natural: aim at satisfying the common sense of those who read and hear, and then, though any one who has no better employment may pick holes in every third sentence, you will have written better English than one who suffers the tyranny of small critics to cramp the expression of his thoughts.

Note after a tithe dinner. 176. The following note has been sent me, received after a tithe dinner in Devonshire : " Mr. T. presents his compliments to Mr. H., and I have got a hat that is not his, and if he have got a hat that is not yours, no doubt they are the expectant ones." It would defy any analysis to detect the source of confusion here. Perhaps "*he*" and "*his*" refer to some third person, not the Mr. H. who is addressed. But I fear we must look for the clue in the notice, "after a tithe dinner." Evidently, the effects of the banquet had not passed away.

Clerical advertisement. 177. The following clerical advertisement from a well-known paper has been sent by a correspondent : " A married A.B., now holding a sole charge, will be disengaged on 17th September. He is an extempore preacher of the doctrines of grace in all their sanctifying influence, and now seeks another." If the hearers of the advertiser fare the same as his readers, I fear the influence, however good, would not be very effectively administered. For it really costs no little ingenuity to discover that it is not another *doctrine* nor another *influence* which he wants, but another *sole charge.*

178. Here is another specimen, in this case an extract from a criticism of Mr. Fechter's "Hamlet," in a daily paper: "His whole system consists in playing the character upside down. He does not ignore tradition, but employs it so far that it enables him to do precisely the reverse. Dress, gait, action, everything, like his pronunciation, are alike unintelligible." This is indeed a delightful specimen of confusion, and obscurity, and bad English. What is *precisely the reverse* which his employment of tradition enables him to do? The reverse of what? Is it the reverse of ignoring tradition? Does the critic mean, that he employs tradition so far that it enables him not to ignore it? Surely this is not the meaning. After feeling about in the

Criticism of Fechter's "Hamlet."

dark some time, we arrive at a sort of suspicion, that the meaning must be, that Mr. Fechter employs tradition so far, that it furnishes him with the means of flying in the face of tradition—of contradicting the whole scope and tenor of tradition—of doing, in fact, precisely the reverse of that which an actor would do who scrupulously followed tradition. Bad as this sentence is, it might be matched ten times over any day on the table of a reading-room.

The same term in different cases. 178*a*. Can we, in an elliptic sentence, use the same term, once only expressed, as doing duty both in the nominative and accusative cases? The late famous Oxford Declaration of the Clergy described the Canonical Scriptures as "not only containing but being the Word of God." The *meaning* was sufficiently clear : but is the phrase correct? I venture to think that it is not, and that it should rather have been said "not only containing the Word of God, but themselves being the Word of God." Both precision and propriety are thus better secured.

178*b*. Indeed we may venture to lay it down as a rule, that in sentences where several forms of speech converge, so to speak, on one term, that term is better expressed or indicated after each of them, than reserved to be expressed or indicated once only at the end of all. "He not only requested an introduction to, but received with the utmost courtesy, placed himself by the side of, and from that day kept up friendly intercourse with, my young protégé," is far better written, "He not only requested an introduction to my young protégé, but received him with the utmost courtesy, placed himself by his side, and from that day kept up friendly intercourse with him." In this sentence, the change for the better is obvious : in many others, constructed in the former manner, it may not be so plain : but that the change is for the better, if judiciously made, will I think in every case be ultimately apparent.

179. Much has been said by my various correspondents about the placing of adverbs and other qualifying terms* in respect of the verbs or nouns with which they are connected ; and the dispute has turned especially on the situation of the adverb "*only*," with regard to its verb. "*Did you see a man and a woman?*" "*No ; I only saw a man.*" This is our ordinary colloquial English. Is it wrong? Of

Position of adverbs : "only."

---

* See this expression justified below, paragraph 181.

course the pedant comes down on us, and
says, "Yes; it is wrong. You want your
adverb '*only*' to qualify, not your act of
seeing, but the number of persons whom you
saw. The proper opposition to '*I only saw
a man*' would be '*I saw and heard a man,*'
or '*I saw and touched him.*'" So far the
pedant; now for common sense. Common
sense at once replies, "I beg the pedant's
pardon; he says I didn't want the adverb
'*only*' to qualify my act of seeing. I say, I
did. For what was the act of seeing? The
two things to be opposed are two acts of
seeing. Seeing a man, and seeing a man and
a woman. It was not the same sight. I only
performed the one; I did not go further, and
perform the other. I only saw a man; I did
not see a man and a woman." Of course the
other way is right also, and, strictly speaking,
the more technically exact of the two; but it
by no means follows that the more exact expression is also the better English. Very
often we cannot have exactness and smooth-
ness together. Wherever this is the case, the
harsher method of constructing the sentence
is, in colloquial English, abandoned, even at
the risk of exactness and school rules. The
adverb "*only*," in many sentences where

strictly speaking it ought to follow its verb and to limit the objects of the verb, is in good English placed before the verb.

180. Let us take an example of this from the great storehouse of good English, our authorised version of the Scriptures. In Ps. lxii. 4, we read, "They only consult to cast him down from his excellency;" *i.e.*, their consultation is on one subject only, how to cast him down. See also Matt. xiv. 36.

181. The account of the matter before us is just this : I may use my adverb *"only"* where two things are spoken of which are affected by the same action, to qualify the one as distinguished from the other, or I may, if I will, separate the action into two parts, the one having regard to the one thing acted on, and the other having regard to the other; and I may make use of my adverb to qualify one part of the action as compared with the other. If I say, " *I will state only one thing more,*" I mean, that being about to state, I will confine that action to one thing and not extend it to any more ; if I say, " *I will only state one thing more,*" I mean that all I will do is, to make one statement, not more. But our gentlemen with their rules never look

about to see whether usage is not justified; they find a sentence not arranged as their books say it ought to be, and it is instantly set down as wrong, in spite of the common sense and practice of all England being against them.

"both." 182. This last-mentioned adverb is not the only word whose position is thus questioned: "*both*" is another. This word, we are told, should always be placed strictly before the former of the words to which it belongs in the sentence, not before the verb or noun which applies equally to the two. Thus, if I say "*They broke down both the door of the stable and of the cellar,*" I am charged with having violated the rules of good English. The pedant would have it, "*They broke down the door both of the stable and of the cellar.*" Now, to my mind, the difference between these two sentences is, that the former is plain collo-quial English: the latter is harsh and cramped, and could not have been written by a sensible man, but only by a man who thought less about conveying the sense of what he said, than about the rules by which his expression should be regulated. But let us see how the great masters of our English tongue wrote. Let us balance Shakspeare against Lindley Murray. In the "Tempest," act i. scene 2, Prospero tells Miranda that the usurping Duke of Milan, her uncle,

> " Having both the key
> Of officer and office, set all hearts i' th' state
> To what tune pleased his ear."

This is, of course, a clear violation of the rule; according to which the words ought to have run, " *having the key of both officer and office.*"

183. As connected with the question of the arrangement of words, I may mention that I have been in controversy, first and last, with several people,* while I have been engaged on my edition of the Greek Testament, about the expression " *the three first Gospels.*" My correspondents invariably maintain that this expression, which I always use, must be an oversight, and that I ought to say " *the first three Gospels.*" I should like to argue this out ; and the present seems a good opportunity for doing so.

" The three first Gospels.'

184. There are Four Gospels, as we all know. And such is the distinctive character of the three which are placed first, as compared with the one which is placed last, that it often becomes necessary to speak of the

* See paragraph 318*a*, below.

L

three, and the one, in two separate classes. It is in doing so that I say "*the three first Gospels*," and my correspondents want me to say "*the first three Gospels*." Which of the two is right? or, if both are right, which of the two is the better?

185. My view is this. The whole number is divided into two classes: the *first* class, and the *last* class. To the former of these belong three: to the latter belongs one. There are three that are ranged under the description "*first:*" and there is one that is ranged under the description "*last.*" Just in this way are the two classes spoken of in that saying of our Lord, "There are last which shall be first, and there are first which shall be last." (Luke xiii. 30.) It is not necessary that *one only* should be spoken of as first, and *one only* as last, as this quotation shows. The whole class is first, as compared with the whole other class which is last. Of twelve persons I may make two classes, and speak of the *five first*, and the *seven last*. This is a correct and logical way of speaking. The opposition between the two classes is as strict and complete, as when I say that of twelve men there are five tall and seven short. If then I wish to divide twelve men into two

classes, I say, and I maintain I say rightly, *the five first* and *the seven last.* If I wish to divide the four Gospels into two classes, I say, and maintain I say rightly, the *three first* Gospels, and the last Gospel.

186. Now let us try the correctness of the other expression, "*the first three Gospels.*" Used in common talk, it would of course convey the same idea as the other. But that is not our present question. Our question is, which of the two is the more precise and correct? When I say "*the first three,*" the idea presented to the mind is, that I am going to speak of *another three,* which shall be set in contrast to them. The proper opposition to "*a tall man*" is "*a short man,*" not a short *stick.* When therefore I take twelve men, and dividing them into two classes, speak of the tall five and the short seven, I may be intelligible, but I certainly am not speaking precisely nor properly. And so when I take four Gospels, and, dividing them into two classes, speak of "*the first three,*" and "*the last one,*" I may be complying with technical rules, but I maintain that I am not complying with the requirements of common sense, and therefore neither with those of good English.

187. A correspondent writes :—"As to the *'three first Gospels,'* your explanation is clear. But would it be right to say, 'in the *three first weeks* of the quarter, the receipts were below the average?' and if not, why not?" In my opinion, it would be perfectly right to speak thus ; and in the particular instance given, "the three first weeks" would be better than "the first three weeks," for another reason ; that "*three weeks*" being a not unusual designation of the portion of time extending over three weeks, the expression, "the first three weeks" would fail to direct the attention to the receipts week by week, which appears to be the desire of the speaker.

Confused use of "he" and "it."

188. Fault has been found with me by some of my correspondents and censors, for the confused use, as they are pleased to regard it, of the personal pronouns "he" and "it." Now here is another matter on which they and I are entirely at issue. A rule is cited from Dr. Campbell, that "wherever the pronoun 'he' will be ambiguous, because two or more males happen to be mentioned in the same clause of a sentence, we ought always to give another turn to the expression, or to use the noun itself and not the pronoun : for

when the repetition of a word is necessary, it is not offensive. The translators of the Bible," continues Dr. C., " have often judiciously used this method : I say judiciously, because though the other method be on some occasions preferable, yet, by attempting the other they would have run a much greater risk of destroying " (he means, " a much greater risk, namely, that of destroying") " that beautiful simplicity which is an eminent characteristic of Holy Writ. I shall take an instance from the speech of Judah to his brother Joseph in Egypt : ' We said to my lord, the lad cannot leave his father, for if he should leave his father, his father would die.' The words ' his father' are in this short verse thrice repeated, and yet are not disagreeable, as they contribute to perspicuity. Had the last part of the sentence run thus : ' if he should leave his father he would die,' it would not have appeared from the expression whether it was the child or the parent that would die."

189. So far Dr. Campbell, " Philosophy of Rhetoric." Now it so happens, that although Dr. Campbell has been able to find an instance to illustrate his point, this is a matter about which the translators of the Bible, and indeed the best of our English writers, *care very*

little; of this, numerous instances might be produced out of our English Bible. I will content myself with two : the first from 2 Kings i. 9 : "Then the king sent unto him a captain of fifty with his fifty : and he went up to him : and behold, he sat on the top of an hill." To common sense it is plain enough who is meant in each case by *he* and *him,* and I don't suppose a mistake was ever made about it : but the sentence is in direct violation of Dr. Campbell's rule. Again, in Luke xix. 3, 4, we read of Zaccheus : "And he sought to see Jesus who he was ; and could not for the press, because he was little of stature. And he ran before, and climbed up into a sycamore tree to see him : for he was to pass that way." Now here you see the pronouns "*he*" and "*him*" are used indiscriminately, sometimes of our Lord, sometimes of Zaccheus : and yet every one knows to whom to apply each of them. The caviller might find ambiguity over and over again ; and accordingly one of my censors says of this very example, "you surely do not defend the construction of these sentences ?" All I can tell him is, they run thus in the *original :* and this, our translators very well knew, is not a matter of the grammar of *our* language, but of all languages, belonging in fact to the laws of human thought. As to the translators having, as Dr. Campbell says, often judiciously used the other method, the expression is peculiarly unfortunate. Our translators rendered most commonly what they found in the original, and very rarely indeed would have thought of repeating the noun where the original had the pronoun. In the example from Genesis, it would have been better if they had not repeated the words "his father" the third time, but had left the sentence ambiguous, as I believe it is in the original Hebrew.*

* The Edinburgh Reviewer (July, 1864), in treating with just contempt the objections of these eager discoverers of ambiguities, makes the following very sensible remarks : "If a man writes in a way which cannot be misunderstood by a reader of common candour and intelligence, he has done all, as regards clearness, that can be expected of him. To attempt more is to ask of language more than language can perform : the consequences of attempting it any one may see who will spend an hour with the Statutes at large. Jack was very respectful to Tom, and always took off his hat when he met him. Jack was very rude to Tom, and always knocked off his hat when he met him. Will any one pretend that either of these sentences is ambiguous in meaning, or unidiomatic in expression? Yet critics of the class now before us are bound to contend that Jack showed his respect by taking off Tom's hat, or else that he showed his rudeness by knocking off his own. It is use-

190. What are we to think of the question, whether "*than*" does or does not govern an accusative case? "*than I :*" "*than me :*" which is right? My readers will probably answer without hesitation, the former. But is the latter so certainly wrong? We are accustomed to hear it stigmatised as being so; but I think, erroneously. Milton writes, "Paradise Lost," ii. 299,

> Which when Beelzebub perceived, than whom,
> Satan except, none higher sat.

And thus every one of us would speak : "than who" would be intolerable. And this seems to settle the question.

191. The fact is, that there are two ways of

less to multiply examples; no book was ever written that could stand a hostile examination in this spirit : and one that could stand it would be totally unreadable."

I will add a story serving to show the usefulness, on certain occasions, of these penny-wise grammarians. The churchwardens of a parish near Bristol, having reason to make a presentation to the Bishop, met to draw it up. Churchwarden A brought the draft, beginning, "My Lord . . ." But Churchwarden B was a man of education, with the rules of grammar ever on his tongue. "My" was of course incorrect, where the "presentors" were two persons. The presentation, he maintained, ought to be corrected; and it narrowly escaped going up to the Bishop addressed to him as "*Our Lord* . . ."

constructing a clause with a comparative and
"*than.*" You may say either "*than I*" or
"*than me.*" If you say the former, you use
what is called an elliptical expression : *i.e.*,
an expression in which something is left out ;
—and that something is the verb "*am.*"
"He is wiser than I," being filled out, would
be, "He is wiser than I am :" "He is wiser
than me," is the direct and complete construction. The difference between the two usages
seems to be this : and it is curiously confirma-
tive of what has been sometimes observed,
that men in ordinary converse shrink, in certain cases, from the use of the bare nominative
of the personal pronoun. Where solemnity
is required, the construction in the nominative is used. Our Lord's words will occur to
us (John xiv. 28), "My Father is greater
than I." But in ordinary conversation this
construction is generally avoided, as sounding
too weighty and formal. In colloquial talk
we commonly say either "He is older than
me," or perhaps more frequently, "He is
older than I am." And so with the other
personal pronouns, *he, she, we,* and *they.*

Still it is urged that "than me" cannot be
right : or can only be right when "me" is
necessarily in government, as in the sentence,

"He likes you better than me." I can do no more in reply, than urge the necessity of saying, "than whom," to show that "*than*" can and does really govern an objective case by its own power, and therefore may govern "me," or "him," or "her," or "them," if we choose so to construct the sentence.

"It is me." 192. The mention of the nominative and accusative of the personal pronoun seems not inaptly to introduce a discussion of the well-known and much controverted phrase, "It is me." Now this is an expression which every one uses. Grammarians (of the smaller order) protest: schoolmasters (of the lower kind) prohibit and chastise; but English men, women, and children go on saying it, and will go on saying it as long as the English language is spoken. Here is a phenomenon worth accounting for. "Not at all so," say our censors: "don't trouble yourself about it; it is a mere vulgarism. Leave it off yourself, and try to persuade every one else to leave it off."

193. But, my good censors, I cannot. I did what I could. I wrote a letter inviting the chief of you to come to Canterbury and hear my third lecture. I wrote in some fear and trembling. All my adverbs were (what

I should call) misplaced, that I might not offend him. But at last, I was obliged to transgress, in spite of my good resolutions. I was promising to meet him at the station, and I was going to write : " if you see on the platform ' *an old party in a shovel,*' that will be I." But my pen refused to sanction (to *endorse,* I believe I ought to say, but I cannot) the construction. " *That will be me* " came from it, in spite, as I said, of my resolve of the best possible behaviour.*

Dr. Latham's opinion.

194. Let us see what a real grammarian says on the matter : one who does not lay down rules only, but is anxious to ascertain on what usages are founded. Dr. Latham, in his admirable " History of the English Language," p. 586, says, " We may . . . . call the word *me* a secondary nominative : inasmuch as such phrases as *it is me* = *it is I*, are common. To call such expres-

---

* Of course it will be obvious, that in the independently constructed clause "that will be me (or I)," no difference whatever in the case of the personal pronoun can be made by its previous construction in the sentence. The mention of such an idea needs an apology : but it has been actually maintained that the accusative is right in this clause, because the personal pronoun represents a noun governed by the verb "see" : "that will be me [you will see]."

sions incorrect English, is to assume the point. No one says that *c'est moi* is bad French, and *c'est je* is good. The fact is that, with us, the whole question is a question of degree. Has or has not the custom been sufficiently prevalent to have transferred the forms *me*, *ye*, and *you*, from one case to another? Or perhaps we may say, is there any real custom at all in favour of *I*, except so far as the grammarians have made one? It is clear that the French analogy is against it. It is also clear that the personal pronoun as a predicate may be in a different analogy from the personal pronoun as a subject."

195. And in another place, p. 584, he says: "What if the current objections to such expressions as *it is me* (which the ordinary grammarians would change into *it is I*), be unfounded, or rather founded upon the ignorance of this difference (the difference between the use of the pronoun as subject and as predicate)? That the present writer defends this (so-called) vulgarism may be seen elsewhere. It may be seen elsewhere, that he finds nothing worse in it than a Frenchman finds in *c'est moi*, where, according to the English dogma, *c'est je* would be

the right expression. Both constructions, the English and the French, are predicative : and when constructions are predicative, a change is what we must expect rather than be surprised at."

196. The account which Dr. Latham has here given, is doubtless the right one. There is a disposition, when the personal pronoun is used predicatively, to put it into the accusative case. That this is more prevalent in the pronoun of the first person singular than in the others, may perhaps arise from the fact which Dr. Latham has elsewhere established, that *me* is not the proper, but only the adopted accusative of *I*, being in fact a distinct and independent form of the personal pronoun. But, it may fairly be asked, whence arises this disposition to shrink from the use of the nominative case in the predicate ? For it does not apply to all instances where the pronoun is predicative. " He said unto them, it is I : be not afraid." This is a capital instance : for it shows us at once why the nominative should be sometimes used. The Majesty of the Speaker here, and His purpose of re-assuring the disciples by the assertion that it was none other than Himself, at once point out to us the case in which it would be

proper for the nominative, and not the accusative, to be used.*

"it is him," "it is her."

197. Dr. Latham goes on to say, after the first of my two citations, p. 587, "At the same time it must be observed, that the expression, *it is me = it is I,* will not justify the use of *it is him, it is her = it is he,* and *it is she. Me, ye, you,* are what may be called *indifferent* forms, *i.e.,* nominative as much as accusative, and accusative as much as nominative. *Him* and *her,* on the other hand, are not indifferent. The -*m* and -*r* are respectively the signs of cases other than the nominative."

198. But is this quite consistent with the idea that the categorical use of the pronoun in the predicate may be different from that of the same pronoun as a subject? *Me* may not have been the original accusative case of *I:* but it is unquestionably the adopted accusative, in constant use as such. Where lies the difference, *grammatically,* between *it is me,* and *it is him,* or *it is her,* as far as present usage is concerned? It seems to me that, if we are prepared to defend the one, we ought in consistency also to defend the other. When,

* The predicate in the *question,* "Is it I?" (Matt. xxvi. 22), is hardly perhaps a case in point.

in the Ingoldsby legend, the monks of Rheims saw the poor anathematised jackdaw appear, "Regardless of grammar, they cried out, 'That's him!'" And I fear we must show an equal disregard of *what ordinarily passes for grammar*, if we would give a correct account of the prevalent usages of our language.*

199. There is one form of construction which is sometimes regarded as coming under the present question, but with which, in fact, it is not concerned. I mean that occurring in such phrases as "*You didn't know it to be me*," "*I suspected it to be him.*" In these, the accusative cases are simply in government, and nominatives would be altogether ungrammatical. The verb substantive takes the same case after it as went before it. It is in fact, in these [sentences, equivalent to *as*, or *as being*. "*You didn't know it to be I*," would be equivalent to "*you didn't recognise it as I*," which of course would be wrong.

199*a*. A correspondent asks me to notice "a usage now becoming prevalent among persons who ought to know better : viz. that of 'you and I,' after prepositions governing the accusative." He gives an instance from "Bothwell," a poem by Professor Aytoun, p. 199 :

"you and I," accusative.

* See note F, at the end of the volume.

> "But it were vain for you and I
> In single fight our strength to try."

On the impropriety of this there can of course be only one opinion. "Perhaps," my correspondent adds, "Professor Aytoun may have read 'John Gilpin,' and, innocent himself of cockneyisms, may have supposed that it is good English to say

> ' On horseback after *we*.' "

"*as thee*." 199*b*. When Thomson, in "Rule Britannia," wrote "The nations not so blest as thee," was he writing correct English? I venture to think he was. *As*, like *than*, is capable of being used in two distinct constructions, the elliptic, and the complete. "*As thou*" is the elliptic construction, requiring the verb substantive for its completion, "*as thou art*." "*As thee*," like "than whom," is the complete construction, in which the conjunction of comparison has a quasi-prepositional force, and governs the pronoun in the objective case. The construction cited from Sir Walter Scott by one of my critics as faulty,

> "Yet oft in Holy Writ we see
> Even such weak minister as me
> May the oppressor bruise,"

is perfectly correct : not, it is true, the usual form of expression, or the more elegant, but one to which, on purely grammatical grounds, there is no objection. The attempt which my critic makes to convict it of error by assuming it to be the elliptical form, *such . . . as me* (am), only shows how much some of us need reminding of the first principles of the syntax of our language.

200. We have said something of superfluous Use of "of." prepositions : let us remark on the use of prepositions themselves. The preposition "*of*" is sometimes hardly dealt with. When I read in an article in the *Times*, on a late annexation, "What can the Emperor possibly want of these provinces of Savoy?" I saw at once that the writer must be a native of the midland counties, where your friends complain that you have not "*called of them of a long time.*" Now in this case it is not the expression, but the sense meant to be conveyed by it, that is objectionable. "What can the Emperor want of these provinces?" is very good English, if we mean "What request has he to make of these provinces?" But if we mean, as the *Times'* writer evidently did, "What does he *want with* the provinces?" *i.e.*, "What need has he of them?" then it is a vulgarism.

M

201. There is a peculiar use of prepositions, which is allowable in moderation, but must not be too often resorted to. It is the placing them at the end of a sentence, as I have just done in the words "resorted to;" as is done in the command, "Let not your good be evil spoken of;" and continually in our discourse and writing.

Prepositions at the end of sentences.

202. The account to be given of this is, that the preposition, which the verb usually takes after it, is regarded as forming a part of the word itself. To *speak of*, to *resort to*, are hardly verbs and prepositions, but form in each case almost one word. But let us go on. "Where do you come from?" is the only way of putting that inquiry. "Whence come you?" is of course pedantic, though accurate. "Where are you going to?" is exactly like the other question, but here we usually drop the "*to*," merely because the adverb of rest "*where*," has come to be used for the adverb of motion "*whither*," and therefore the "*to*" is not wanted. If a man chooses, as West-country men mostly do, to say "Where are you going to?" he does not violate propriety, though he does violate custom. But let us go further still. *Going to* has not only a *local*, it has also a mental

meaning, being equivalent to *intending* in the mind. And this usage rests on exactly the same basis as the other. The "*to*" of the infinitive mood is precisely the same preposition as the "*to*" of motion towards a place. "Were you going to do it?" simply means "Were you, in your mental intention, approaching the doing of it?" And the proper conversational answer to such a question is, "I was going to," or "I was not going to," as the case may be; not "I was going," or "I was not going," inasmuch as the mere verb *to go* does not express any mental intention. I know, in saying this, that I am at variance with the rules taught at very respectable institutions for enabling young ladies to talk unlike their elders; but this I cannot help; and I fear this is an offence of which I have been, and yet may be, very often guilty.

203. This kind of colloquial abbreviation of the infinitive comprehends several more phrases in common use, and often similarly objected to, *e. g.*, "*ought to*," and "*ought not to*," "*neglect to*," &c., some of them not very elegant, but all quite unobjectionable on the score of grammar. These abbreviations are very common in the West of England,

and are there carried further than any reason
will allow.

204. In many cases of this kind we have
a choice whether the preposition shall precede
or follow the object of the sentence. Thus
I may say, "*the man to whom I had written*,"
or "*the man whom I had written to*." In this
particular instance, the former is the more
elegant, and would usually be said: but this is
not always so ; *e.g.*, "*You're the man I wanted
to have some talk with*," would always be said ;
not, "*You're the man with whom I wanted to
have some talk*," which would sound stilted
and pedantic.

Present,
past, and
perfect
tenses.

205. The next thing I shall mention, not
for its own sake, but as a specimen of the
kind of criticism which I am often meeting
with, and as instructive to those who wish to
be critics of other men's language. I have
said that "Dr. Donne preach*es*" so and so.
My correspondent takes exception to this, and
tells me that Dr. Donne has been dead some
two hundred years, and therefore I ought
to say Dr. Donne *preached*, and not *preaches*.
This may seem mere trifling: but it is worth
while to notice, that we speak thus, in the
present tense, of writings permanently placed
on record. Their authors, being dead, yet

speak to us. It would be affected and unusual to speak otherwise of things cited from books. If we use the past tense at all, it is not the indefinite, but the perfect, which also conveys the idea of a living and acting even now. I should say, "Dr. Donne *has explained* this text thus or thus;" not "Dr. Donne *explained* this text thus or thus." This latter sentence would bear a different meaning. If I say, " Livy *writes*," or " Livy *has written*, so and so," I imply that the book containing the incident is now extant. But if I say, "Livy *wrote* so and so," I should naturally be taken to be speaking of something reported as having been written in one of the books of his history which have been lost. You may say of a sick man yet living, "He has lost much strength during the week." But the moment he is dead, you can no longer thus speak : you must say, "He lost much strength during the week." If I say, " I have seen Wales twice," I carry the period during which my assertion is true through my whole life down to the present time. If I say, " I saw Wales twice," my words simply refer to the fact, and the period to which they refer is understood to have terminated. I mean, in my youth, or when I was in Cheshire, or the like. Sometimes the difference between the two tenses may convey an interesting moral distinction. If I say, "My father left me an injunction to do this or that," I leave the way open to say, "but now circumstances have changed, and I find another course more advisable :" if I say "My father has left me an injunction to do this or that," I imply that I am at this moment obeying, and mean to obey, that injunction. The perfect tense is in fact a present, relating to the effect, at the present time, of some act done in the past.*

Their con-
fusio

206. An important difference in meaning is sometimes made by the wrong or careless use of one of these tenses for the other. An instance of this occurs in the English version of the Bible in the beginning of Acts xix. There we read, in the original, that St. Paul finding certain disciples at Ephesus, asked them, "Did ye receive the Holy Ghost when ye believed—when ye first became believers?" To this they answered, "We did not so much as hear whether there were any Holy Ghost."

---

* The confusion between these tenses is sometimes curious. "I call," says an Irish correspondent, "at the office of a gentleman who is expected every minute, and am told, 'He didn't come to-day,' or, 'He didn't come yet.'"

On which St. Paul asked them, "Unto what then were ye baptized?" They replied, "Unto the baptism of John." Then he explained to them that John's baptism, being only a baptism of repentance, did not bring with it the gift of the Holy Ghost. In this account, all is clear. But the English version, by an unfortunate mistake, has rendered the narrative unintelligible. It has made St. Paul ask the converts, "Have ye received the Holy Ghost since ye believed?" So far, indeed, all would be clear; for they certainly had not, though this does not represent what was said by the Apostle. But it is their answer which obscures the history. "We have not so much as heard," they are made to say, "whether there be any Holy Ghost." Strange indeed, that these disciples, who had probably been for years in the Church, should during that time, and up to the time when St. Paul spoke, never have heard of the existence of the Holy Spirit. Render the words accurately, and all is clear.

207. I am now going to speak of a combination of words which is so completely naturalised, that it would be vain to protest against it, or even to attempt to disuse it one's self. I mean, the joining together of a present and

"was being written."

a past participle, as we do when we say "*The letter was being written*," "*The dinner is being cooked.*" Such combinations were, I believe, not used by our best and most careful writers, until a comparatively recent date. The old and correct way of expressing what is meant by these phrases, was, "*The letter was in writing*," or "*was writing;*" "*The dinner is cooking:*" the verbs being used in a neuter sense. The objection to "*being written*" for "*in the process of writing*," is this,—that "*written*" is a past participle, indicating a finished act. When I say "*I have written a letter*," I mean, I have by me, or have as my act accomplished, a letter written. So that "*being written*" properly means, existing in a state of completion. "*My letter being written, I put it in the post.*" And, strictly speaking, we cannot use the combination to signify an *incomplete* action. Still, as I have said, the inaccuracy has crept into the language, and is now found everywhere, in speech and in writing. The only thing we can do in such a case is to avoid it, where it can be avoided without violation of idiom, or giving harshness to the sentence.

"shall" and "will."

208. The next point which I notice shall be the use of the auxiliaries "*shall*" and "*will.*" Now

here we are at once struck by a curious phenomenon. I never knew an Englishman who misplaced "*shall*" and "*will*:" I hardly ever have known an Irishman or a Scotchman who did not misplace them sometimes. And it is strange to observe how incurable the propensity is. It was but the other day that I asked a person sprung of Irish blood, whether he would be at a certain house to which I was going that evening. The answer was, "*I'm afraid I won't.*" Yet my friend is a sound and accurate English scholar, and I had never before, during all the years I had known him, discovered any trace of the sister island.

209. In attempting to give an explanation of our English usage, I may premise that it is exceedingly difficult to do so. We seem to proceed rather on instinct, than by any fixed rule. Yet instinct, in rational beings, must be founded on some inherent fitness of things; and examination ought to be able to detect that fitness. Let us try to do this, though it may be difficult, in the case before us.

210. The simplest example that can be given "I will." is "*I will.*" Now this can have but one meaning. It can only be used as expressing determination: only, where the will of the person

speaking is concerned. "Wilt thou have this woman to thy wedded wife?" Answer, "I will" (in the Latin, "*volo*"). We cannot use "*I will*," where a mere contingent future event is concerned. We cannot use "*I will*" of anything uncertain, anything about which we hope or fear. "Help me, I'll fall," if strictly interpreted, would be an entreaty to be saved from an act of wilful precipitation. "*I fear I won't*" is an impossible and unmeaning junction of terms. If it meant anything, it could only be, "I fear that, when the time comes, my power of volition will be found too weak for its work." But this is obviously not what it is intended to mean. The account then of "*I will*" seems very simple.

"I shall." 211. Now, what is "*I shall?*" In its ordinary use, it just takes those cases of things future, where "*I will*" cannot be said: those cases where the things spoken of are independent of our own will. "*Next Tuesday I shall be twenty-one*"—an event quite out of my now power. So far, all is plain. But there is a case of "*I shall*" which somewhat complicates the matter. We are in the habit, when announcing something which we positively mean to do, to speak of it as if it were

taken, so to say, out of the region of our own
will, and placed among things absolutely certain ; and in such cases we turn "*will*" into
"*shall.*" The traveller meets with incivility,
or he cannot find his luggage, at the station.
He breaks forth, in angry mood, "*I shall
write to the 'Times' about this,*"—and he
means the station-master to conclude that his
writing is as certain as if it were already
done. The "*shall*" is intended to elevate
the "*will*" into the category of things indis-
putable.

212. So far then for "*will*" and "*shall*" "you will."
when used in the first person. But how when
used in the second ? Let us take "*You will.*"
"*You will*" is used when speaking to another person of a matter entirely out of the
speaker's power and jurisdiction. "*You will
be twenty-one next Tuesday.*" "*If you climb
that ladder you will fall.*" This is the ordinary use. Here again there is an exception,
which I cannot well treat till I have spoken
of "*You shall.*"

213. "*You shall*" or "*You shall not*" is "you shall."
said to another, when the will of the speaker
compels that which is spoken of. "*Thou
shalt love the Lord thy God.*" "*Thou shalt
not steal.*"

Exceptions. 214. The exceptions to both these usages may be stated thus, and they are nearly related to that of which I spoke when on the first person. A master writes to his servant, "*On the receipt of this you will go,*" or "*you will please to go,*" "*to such a place.*" This is treating the obedience of the servant as a matter of certainty, sure to follow of course on his lord's command. The exception in the use of "*shall*" is when we say, for instance, "*If you look through History, you shall find that it has always been so,*" and the account of it seems to be, that the speaker feels as perfect a certainty of the result, as if it were not contingent, but depended only on his absolute command.

"will" and "shall" in the third person. 215. It remains that we consider the words "*will*" and "*shall*" as applied in the third person; said of persons and things spoken about. And here, what has already been said will be a sufficient guide in ordinary cases. For all announcements of common events foreseen in the future, "*will*" is the word to be used. "*I think it will rain before night.*" "*To-morrow will be old May-day.*" We may sometimes use "*shall,*" but it can only be in cases where our own will, or choice, or power, exercises some influence over the events spoken of: as for instance, "*The sun shall not set to-night before I find out this matter.*" "*Next Tuesday shall be the day.*" Notice, you would not say, "*Next Tuesday shall be my birthday:*" you must say, "*Next Tuesday will be my birthday:*" because that is a matter over which you have no control: but the Queen might say, "*Next Tuesday shall be my birthday:*" because she would mean, "*shall be kept as my birthday,*" a matter over which she has control.

216. There are some very delicate and curious cases of the almost indifferent usage of the two auxiliary verbs. Take this one, "*If he will look, he will find it to be so.*" Here we use the first "*will*" in the sense of "*choose to:*" "*If he please to look.*" But the second has its mere future use: "*he will find that it is so.*" Here however we might use, though it would be somewhat pedantic English, the word "*shall*" in both members of the sentence: "*If he shall look, he shall find it to be so,*" and then the former "*shall*" would be in the sense of a mere future, and the second in that sense of absolute certainty, "*I will undertake that he shall find,*" of which I spoke just now. This sentence might in fact be correctly said in four different ways:

Instances of almost indifferent usage.

If he will look, he will find :
If he shall look, he shall find :
If he will look, he shall find :
If he shall look, he will find.

I may mention that the almost uniform use of *"shall"* as applied to future events and to persons concerned in them, is reserved for the prophetic language of the Bible, as spoken by One whose will is supreme and who has all under his control.

217. There are certain other cases in which we may say either *"will"* or *"shall."* In reporting what another said, or what one said one's self, we may say, *"He told me he should go up to town to-morrow and settle it ;"* or we may say, *"He told me he would go up to town,"* &c. This arises from the possibility, already noticed, of using either word in speaking in the first person.

Ambiguity. 218. Sometimes an ambiguity arises from the fact that *"will"* and *"would"* either may convey the idea of inclination of the will, or may point to a mere future event. We have two notable instances in the English version of the New Testament. Our Lord says to the Jews (John v. 40), *"Ye will not come to me that ye might have life."* Is He merely announcing a fact, or is He speaking of the bent and inclination of their minds? We consult the original, and the question is at once answered. What our Lord says, is this: "*Ye are not willing,*" "*ye have no mind,*" "*to come to me that ye might have life.*"

219. Again (Matt. xi. 27). "*No man knoweth the Father save the Son, and he to whomsoever the Son will reveal Him.*" Is this "*will*" a mere auxiliary for the future meaning, or does it convey the idea of *exercise of will?* Here again the original sets us right in a moment. It is, "he to whom the Son is minded to reveal Him."

220. Let us take a still more remarkable case. The Pharisees said to our Lord (Luke xiii. 31), "Get thee hence, for Herod will kill thee." This seems a mere future, and I have no doubt English readers universally regard it as such : but the original is "Herod wishes," "is minded," "to kill thee."

221. The sense of duty conveyed by "*should*" sometimes causes ambiguity. Thus we have (Matt. xxvi. 35), "*Though I should die with thee, yet will I not deny thee.*" This, to the mere English reader, only conveys the sense, "*Even if it should happen that I should die with thee.*" But on consulting the original we find we should be wrong in

thus understanding it. It is "*Even if it be
necessary for me to die with thee*"—and
would have been better rendered, "*Even if I
must die with thee.*" But in another clause
(John xxi. 19), "*This spake He, signifying
by what death he should glorify God,*" the
"*should*" does not represent any necessity,
but the mere future.

222. Which is right, "*it would seem,*" or
"*it should seem*"? asks a Scottish correspondent. I believe both are right, but
with slightly differing meanings. Both, be it
observed, are expressions of very slight and
qualified assent. The former, "*it would
seem,*" implies, "we are told that if we were
to weigh all that is to be said, we should
come to such or such a conclusion." The
latter, "*it should seem,*" conveys the meaning,
with perhaps a slightly ironical tinge, that
we are *required* to believe so and so. The
Germans use their "*soll,*" in reporting the
conclusions or belief of others, in nearly the
same sense.

223. An amusing instance of the confusion
of *shall* and *will* was repeated to me by
another Scottish correspondent. A young
men's "Institute for Discussion and Self-
improvement" is reported in a Scottish pro-

"it would
seem," "it
should
seem."

Confusion of
"shall" and
"will."

vincial paper to have met, and discussed the question, "Shall the material universe be destroyed?" My correspondent supposes that the decision was in the negative : or that if it was in the affirmative, the society cannot have proceeded to carry its resolution into effect.

224. I believe Dr. Latham, in his "History of the English Language," was the first to observe that the confusion in such cases is more apparent than real. The Englishman and the Scotchman mean the same thing, but express it differently. We may say either, "the material universe *will* be destroyed," expressing merely something which will happen some day in the future : or we may say "the material universe *shall* be destroyed," in which case we put more solemnity and emphasis into our announcement, and treat it as something inevitable, pronouncing almost as if we were exercising our own will in the matter. When we turn the assertion into a question, *we* say, "Will the material universe be destroyed?" the Scotchman says, "Shall the material universe be destroyed?" He means to put, as a question, what we meant, when we used *shall* in the assertion. But be it observed, that in turning the proposition

Dr. Latham's account of this.

N

into a question, the *shall* assumes a ludicrous form, because of the deliberative aspect given to the sentence; and it looks as if the person putting the question had the option whether he would destroy the universe or not.

A case in which it seems to fail.

225. Five years ago I was visiting Loch Maree, in Ross-shire, with my family. We took a "trap" from the comfortable inn at Kinloch-Ewe, and lunched and sketched on the cliffs, about twelve miles down the lake. When our time was nearly up, our Highland driver appeared in the distance, shouting, "Will I yauk him?" which, being interpreted, meant to say, "Shall I harness the pony?" I hardly see how even Dr. Latham's explanation will account for the usage here.*

---

* I venture to insert the following remarks of a very intelligent Irish correspondent :—

" Your rules for the use of '*shall*' and '*will*' seem to me, as far as they go, the most simple and satisfactory I have ever read.   But I observe :—

" I. No rule is laid down for the use of these words in interrogation.   In Ireland the tendency is to make use of 'will' in *every case*.   I have collected several examples from English writers which seem to me to suggest the following rules :—

" ' *Will you?*' is a *request*.

" ' *Shall you?*' a simple *question* as to the future event.

" ' *Will he?*' a simple question.

" ' *Shall he?*' means ' *do you wish* that he shall.'

226. We often find persons using super-fluous conjunctions or prepositions in their

"'*Will I?*' is always incorrect.

"'*Shall I?*' has two meanings: 1st, it asks the simple question as to the future event, *v.g.*, 'shall I be of age next month?' 2nd, it asks, 'do you wish that *I shall?*' *v.g.*, 'shall I call you friend?'

"II. You say nothing of the use of these words in the secondary clauses of such sentences as the following:

"'He hopes that he *shall* not be thought,' &c.

"'He walked into a church knowing well he *should* find,' &c.

"Phrases of this kind occur very frequently, and, I think, almost all my countrymen would be found to use *will* and *would* instead of *shall* and *should*. I may add that, as it seems to me nothing to be found in your book would set them right on this point, I would propose the following principle for such cases :—If we report in our own words what another has said, or thought, or known, or felt, we must use that verb which he would have used if, speaking in the first person, he had himself related the circumstance.

"III. There is to be found almost every day in the *Times* (second column) a curious illustration of the distinction between 'shall' and 'will.' When a person advertises for a lost article we sometimes read, 'If any person brings, &c., he *shall* be rewarded:' sometimes we find, 'a reward *will* be given.' Now here your rules seem to be at fault. The future event, namely, the giving of the reward, is dependent upon the will of the speaker in the latter case as well as in the former. If the rule hold good, therefore, we might say, 'A reward *shall* be given.' Yet this is never said."

[This seems to fall under the list of exceptions mentioned in paragraph 214; where the result is so spoken of as not contingent but certain. "A reward *shall* be

usual talk.* Two cases are more frequent than others. One is the use of *but* after the verb *to doubt.* "I do not doubt *but that* he will come," is both found in print and heard in conversation. The *"but"* is wholly unnecessary, and a vulgarism. "I do not doubt that he will come," expresses precisely the same thing, and should always be used.

"on to."

227. The same may be said of the expression *on to.* "The cat jumped on to the chair;" the *to* being wholly unneeded, and never used by any careful writer or speaker.

Defence of it.

228. Few points mentioned in these "notes" have provoked so much rejoinder as this reprobation of "*on to.*" It seems, to judge by its many defenders, to be an especial favourite. The plea usually set up for it is, that "*on*" without "*to*" does not sufficiently express *motion*: that "the cat jumped on the chair" would imply merely that the cat, being on the chair already, there jumped. To this I have but one answer; that no doubt the words *may* mean this, to one who is disposed to invent meanings for them; but that they *do* mean

given," is the subjective dictum of him who has so determined: "a reward will be given," is the objective future certainty, the *determination* being lost sight of.]

this, is surely not true. "The cat jumped on the table, and began to lap the milk." Who would ever misunderstand this? Take an incident of one's schoolboy long walks. "Coachman, I'm very tired, and I shall be late in; but I've got no money in my pocket." "All right, my lad, jump on the box." Was there ever a schoolboy who would fail to comprehend this?*

229. One correspondent asks why "*on to*" "on to" is not as good English as "*into?*" I answer, because "*on*" is ordinarily a preposition of motion as well as of rest, whereas "*in*" is almost entirely a preposition of rest. To *fall on*, to *light on*, and the like, are very common; and we are thus prepared for the use of *on* to signify motion without an additional preposition.

229*a*. It will be manifest, that the juxta-   "holding on to." position of "*on*" and "*to*" in such a sentence

---

* Since the publication of the first edition, several correspondents have again vehemently controverted the opinion here expressed: and I have been even urged to withdraw it and confess myself in the wrong. I am afraid, therefore, that my correspondents will think me very obstinate for still maintaining my view: and saying, that I cannot conceive what signification of *motion towards* is gained by the vulgarism "*on to*," which is not already conveyed by "*on*," or at all events by "*upon*."

as this, "she continued holding on to the door of the carriage," is not an example within the scope of these remarks. The "*on*" in this case belongs to the verb: and "*holding-on to*" is equivalent to "*clinging to.*"

"on" and "upon."

230. How do our usages of "*on*" and "*upon*" differ? In the very few cases where we recognise any difference, the question may be answered by observing the composition of the latter word. It almost always, as the dictionaries observe, "implies some substratum;" something that underlies the thing spoken of. But then so does also the shorter preposition in most cases. There is hardly an instance to be found of which it could positively be said, that we may use the one preposition and may not use the other. Perhaps we may find one, when we say that a diver, describing his trip beneath the water, would hardly report that he "saw several rusty guns lying *upon* the bottom," but "lying *on* the bottom."

231. A correspondent sends me what he supposes to be an account of the distinction, but I believe it to be an erroneous one. "I would (should?) say, '*upon* a tower;' on the same principle, I would (should?) say, '*on* a marsh.' There would, indeed, be no

harm in saying 'on a tower;' but there would be an impropriety in saying 'upon a marsh;' for *up*, whether we are attentive or inattentive, whether we have been a thousand times wrong or never, means somewhat high, somewhat to which we ascend. I should speak correctly if I said, 'Dr. Johnson *flew* upon me:' incorrectly, if I said, 'he *fell* upon me.'"

232. The error here seems to me to be in referring the height indicated by *up* to the motion previous to, not to the position indicated by, the action spoken of. We perhaps cannot say "*upon* the bottom;" not however because *we* do not *rise* to get there, but because the bottom, being of necessity the lowest point, has nothing beneath it with reference to which it is high. And as to my correspondent's last dictum, that "he fell upon me" would be incorrect, let him look at 1 Kings ii. 25, 34, 46, in which places it is said of Adonijah, Joab, and Shimei, respectively, that Benaiah, the son of Jehoiada, "*fell upon him* that he died."

233. The expression "*to open up*," is a very favourite one with our newspapers. It may have, as several of my correspondents insist, a certain meaning of its own, though

To "open up."

I am even now unable to see, in any case where I have found it, why the simple word "open" would not be better. The meaning which it is designed to convey, seems to be, to open for the first time,—to break up and open. A railway is said to *open up* a communication between two places not so connected before. Thus used, the term may be endured, but, surely, should not be imitated. As to the instances from "Good Words," which have been produced against me as if I were responsible for them, "He *opens up* in the parched desert a well that refreshes us;" "These considerations may *open up* to us one view of the expediency of Christ's departure;" I can only regard them as Scotticisms, which certainly would not have been written south of the Tweed.

234. The parallel which the defenders of the expression have drawn between *open up* and *rise up*, *grow up*, is hardly a just one, seeing that in these cases the adverb, or intransitive preposition, *up*, gives us the tendency in which the progressive action indicated by the neuter verb takes place; and even if it do not that, intensifies and gives precision. More apposite parallels would have been found in *rip up*, *tear up*, *pull*

up, where *up* defines the active verb; a more decisive one still, in the term *to shut up*, where *up* implies the *closing* and *finality* of the act indicated; and for this reason should hardly be used with the opposite word *to open*. If we *shut up* a communication, we ought to *open* it *down* rather than *up*. Put the word with any analogous term, and its inappropriateness will be perceived. A new railway develops, expands, promotes, the traffic; but we could not say it *develops up, expands up, promotes up*, the traffic.

235. Which is right, "at *best*," or "at *the best?*" It is plain that this question does not stand alone; several other phrases are involved in it. It affects "at least," "at most," "at furthest," and even such very common expressions as "at first," and "at last." "at best," "at the best."

The answer, it seems to me, is, that the insertion or omission of the definite article is indifferent. Usage has generally sanctioned its omission before the very common superlatives, "first," "last," "most," "least," "furthest;" but when we put a less usual adjective in this construction, the article seems to be required, or a possessive pronoun in its place. "The storm was at the (or, "its") highest at noon;" "What is woman at her loveliest?" And we sometimes fill out the phrase with the article when we want it to be more than usually solemn: "If he did not love his father, at the least he might have honoured him." "At the last" is found six times in the English Bible; "at last," if we may trust the concordances, never; "at the first," twenty-eight times; "at first," never; "at the least," three times; while "at least" is found twice (1 Sam. xxi. 4, Luke xix. 42); "at the most," once (1 Cor. xiv. 27); but "at most," never.

236. "*All of them*," "*both of them*." These expressions are often challenged. Are they right, or not? When I have a number of things, and speak of "one of them," "two of them," "the rest of them," the preposition "*of*" has what is called its partitive sense. It may be explained by "*out of*," or "*from among*." Thus, "one of them" is "one from among them;" "two of them" is "two from among them;" "the rest of them" is "all from among them that do not belong to those already named." But, it is urged, "all of them" cannot be "all from among them," because there would be none left. Neither

"all of them," "both of them."

can "both of them" be said of two, because when you have taken both, there is nothing left.

237. But let us examine this. Is it so certain that the "of" in the phrases "all of them," "both of them," has the same meaning as the "of" in the phrases "one of them," "two of them," "some of them"? Let us, for "all of them," put "the whole of them," and for that, "the sum total of them," or, as our newspapers would say, "the entirety of them." Now it is manifest that any one of these is good grammar, and that the "of" does not mean "*from among*," but implies "consisting of:" is spoken of the quality, as "sum total," or "entirety," is of quantity. "The sum total of them," is as legitimate as "a pint of beer." Why not, then, "all of them," or "both of them?" The fallacy of the objection here is, the assuming for the preposition a sense which it need not have, just because it had that sense in some phrases apparently similar. In other words, the mistake was, being misled by a false analogy.

237*a.* "A gallows fifty cubits high," or, "a gallows of fifty cubits high"? The former expression is used in Esther vii. 9; the latter "fifty cubits high," or "of fifty cubits high"?

in Esther v. 14. Clearly, both of these are legitimate. A gallows whose height is fifty cubits, may be said to be "fifty cubits high": it is high, and the measure of that height is fifty cubits. Thus we have "a mile wide": "ten thousand fathoms deep." Also, the same gallows may be said to be "of fifty cubits" (high, or, in height) : the "of" being used, as in the phrases "she was of the age of twelve years" (Mark v. 42), "of a great age" (Luke ii. 36), to indicate the class or standard of the object spoken of. The gallows is high, and belongs to that class of things whose height is fifty cubits.

Adverb between "to" and the infinitive.

238. A correspondent states as his own usage, and defends, the insertion of an adverb between the sign of the infinitive mood and the verb. He gives as an instance, "*to scientifically illustrate.*" But surely this is a practice entirely unknown to English speakers and writers. It seems to me, that we ever regard the *to* of the infinitive as inseparable from its verb. And when we have already a choice between two forms of expression, "scientifically to illustrate," and "to illustrate scientifically," there seems no good reason for flying in the face of common usage.

"going" and "coming."

239. In a letter bearing after its address,

"N. B.," I am asked whether the expression "I am *coming* to pay you a visit" is correct: whether it ought not rather to be "I am *going* to pay you a visit:" and the question is extended to the reply, "I am coming," when any one calls; which is also supposed to be incorrect, and still more so when followed by "directly." I mentioned the address of the letter to account in some measure for the inquiry; for it seems to me to be one which we Southrons should never have thought of making. In both cases, *coming* is right. In the former, we might use *going*, but it would be in the temporal sense, not in that of motion. But in the other, we could not say *going* at all, if we indicated approach to the person calling. An apology is almost required for setting down things so simple and obvious; but the doing so may serve to show what sort of usages prevail and are upheld in some portions of our realm.

240. When I used, in the early part of these notes, the colloquial expression *would have come to grief*, I was told by one of my censors that it ought to have been *would have gone to grief*. It is not easy, perhaps, to treat according to strict rule what is almost a slang phrase, or has but lately ceased to be one;

"como to grief."

still, I venture to think that *to come to grief* is
of the two the more according to the analogy
of our usage. We say *to come to an end*, not
to go to an end ; we say of a desperate young
villain, that he will *come to the gallows*, not
that he will *go to the gallows*. Indeed, if
we chose, we might illustrate the difference
between the two expressions, by saying what
I fear is often true of the effect of our public
executions, that *going to the gallows* is but too
likely to end in *coming to the gallows*.

Other uses
of "go" and
"come."

241. This use of *go* and *come* is rather
curious. We say of a wrecked ship, that she
went to pieces ; but of a crushed jug, that it
came to pieces. Plants *come* up, *come* into
leaf, *come* into flower ; but they *go* to seed,
they *go* out of flower. It may be that in
this case we regard the above-ground state as
that in which we ourselves are, and the being
in leaf and in flower as those in which we
wish them to be, and like to think of them ;
and so the passing into those states is a kind
of approach to us : whereas the state of seed
being one leading to decay, and beyond what
is our own place and feeling as regards flowers,
they seem to depart from us in passing into
it. Thus the sun *goes* in behind a cloud, and
comes out from behind it. But we are not

consistent in speaking of the sun. He is said to *go down* in the evening ; but never to *come up* in the morning.

242. And very minute shades of meaning are sometimes conveyed by the use of one or other of these verbs. You are talking about a public meeting with a friend who you know will be there. If you say to him " I shall not *come* to the meeting," you identify him with those who get up the meeting, and imply that he is desirous you should join him there. If you say, " I shall not go to the meeting," you tacitly ignore the fact of his being about to attend, and half imply that he would do well to stay away also. " Are you *coming* to church to-day ? " implies that the questioner *is ;* " Are you *going* to church to-day ? " implies nothing as to whether he is or is not. To this latter question one might rejoin, "Yes : are you ? " but not so to the former.

243. In nothing do we find more frequent mistakes in writers commonly careful, than in using the accusative case of a relative pronoun where the nominative ought to be used. A correspondent, for instance, describing what he thinks the disastrous effects of my advocacy of " *it is me*," says, " I have heard per- misuse of " whom."

sons *whom* I knew were in the habit of using
the form 'it is I,' say instead, 'it is me.'"
Here, the mistake is very evident. "I knew"
is merely parenthetical, put in by way of
voucher for the fact—"persons who, I knew,
were." The writer might have said, "*whom
I knew to be,*" or "*to have been;*" but as the
sentence stands, *who* must be the nominative
case to the verb *were.*

244. A still worse example occurred in the
Times a short time since, in translating the
Count de Montalembert's famous speech in
favour of liberty of conscience. It would
perhaps be hard to criticise a report of a
speech; but the sentence was quoted for especial comment in the leading article, and no
correction was made. It ran thus: "The
gag forced into the mouth of *whomsoever
lifts* up his voice with a pure heart to preach
his faith, that gag I feel between my own
lips, and I shudder with pain."

245. Now in this sentence, first of all it
is clear that "whomsoever lifts" cannot be
right. The indefinite relative pronoun ought
to be the nominative case to the verb lifts,
and therefore ought to be *whosoever* and not
whomsoever.

246. But then, how about the construc-

tion? "The mouth of whosoever lifts" is an elliptical clause. Filled up, it will be "*the mouth of him whosoever lifts,*" or, more completely, "*of him whosoever he be that lifts.*" In its shortened form we have the object, "*him,*" omitted. But we must not visit this omission on the unfortunate relative pronoun which follows, and degrade it from its place in the sentence by making it do the work of the missing member.

247. A correspondent stigmatises the expression "*different to,*" which he shows (I own I was not aware of it) has become very common of late. Of course such a combination is entirely against all reason and analogy. "Compare," says this writer, "any other English words compounded of this same Latin preposition, for example, '*distant*,' '*distinct*,' and it will be seen that '*from*' is the only appropriate term to be employed in connection with them." The same will be seen, I venture to add, by substituting the verb "*to differ*" in the places where "*different,*" which in fact is only its participle, is thus joined. For instance, in the sentence quoted from Mr. Taylor's *Convent Life in Italy*, "Michael Angelo planned a totally different façade to the existing one," make this substi-

"different to

o

tution, and read it, "Michael Angelo planned
a façade which totally differed to the existing
one," and the error will be immediately seen.

248. "*In respect of*," "*in respect to*," "*with
respect to :*" which of these is right? The
question extends also to "*in regard of*," "*in
regard to*," "*with regard to*." For *respect* and
regard, though far from meaning the same
when spoken of as feelings of the mind, yet
in their primitive meaning, which is that now
treated of, are identical.

249. I believe it will be found that *of* and
to may be indifferently used after these words.
Both words have the same signification ; *an
act of looking back at.* The former, *respect*,
is a Latin word, and the expression answering
to "in respect of," is used in Latin. At the
same time, the natural construction of the
verb from which *respect* is derived would be
with the preposition *to* (*respicere ad*). There
is nothing in the meaning of the word to
forbid either construction—with *of*, or with
to. The same may be said of *regard*, which
is of French origin.

250. Still, if we agree on this much, it
remains to be seen what preposition should
be *prefixed*. "*In respect of*" is the pure Latin
construction, and seems on all hands (but see

below) to be admitted as pure English like-wise. And the same with "*in regard of;*" "*with respect to,*" and "*in respect to,*" are both found : the former I think the more frequently in our best writers. But, unless I am mistaken, "*with respect of,*" is not found.

251. When one of my Censors said of a sentence in these notes, that I had used "*in respect of,*" for "*with respect to,*" he surely must have been speaking without his authorities before him. He will find in the dictionaries, that in the scanty lists there given, Spenser, Bacon, Tillotson, all use the expression com-plained of. It occurs in Philippians iv. 11, and Colossians ii. 16, and is certainly as much used by good modern writers as that which he wishes to substitute for it.

252. What the same Censor means when he says that "*inversely as*" should be "*inversely to,*" I am at a loss to understand. I can comprehend "*in inverse proportion to,*" or "*in inverse ratio to ;*" but surely by all the usages of mathematical language, from which the phrase is borrowed, one variable thing must be said to be directly or inversely *as,* not *to,* another which is compared with it. "inversely as."

252*a.* A correspondent asks the question, "*contrast to,*" or "*contrast with ?*" It may "contrast to," or "with."

o 2

be answered that both of these seem allowable. For *contrast* partakes of two ideas; that of *opposition*, and that of *comparison*. Now we oppose one thing *to* another, and we (commonly) compare one thing *with* another. Still, as the idea of opposition is, beyond question, the prevalent one, I should prefer " *contrast to.*"

Meaning of "a term." 253. Nor can I comprehend again what the Censor above-mentioned means when he says, in reference to my-having called an adverb "a term," that an adverb is not a term, but a *word*, a *part of a term*. For the whole account to be given of " *term*," its derivation and its usage, is against him. It comes to us proximately from the Latin *terminus*—directly from the French " *terme*." Both these, when used of language, signify, not a clause, but a *word*. And so our dictionaries give the meaning of the English *term* —"The word by which a thing is expressed."

Reason for mentioning these objections. 254. I mention this, not for the sake of self-vindication, which forms no part of my design in collecting these notes, but that I may guard others against being misled by this incorrect view of the meaning of a word in common use.

"I need not 255. With the same end in view, I notice

another of his objections. "*I need not have* ·have troubled myself."
troubled myself." He would correct this to
"*I should not have needed to trouble myself :*"
saying, "the verb *troubled*, which you have
put in the past, should have been in the present : just as the verb *need*, which you have
put in the present, should have been in the
past." Now in these words appears the cause
of my Censor's mistake. It is the very common one of confusing a *perfect* tense with
a *past* one. "I need not have troubled myself" is strictly correct; being equivalent to
"I need not be in the present situation of
having troubled myself." Every *perfect* is in
fact a *present*. "*I have troubled myself*" describes not a past action, but the *present result*
of a past action. This is now so generally
acknowledged even by the ordinary grammarians, that it is strange in our days to
find any one who attends to the matter
making a mistake about it.

256. Seeing, however, that this has been ·Caution
done, it may be as well to put my readers on ·respecting
·past and
their guard, ever to bear in mind the dis- ·perfect
tinction between the *indefinite past* and the ·tenses.
perfect. I have said something on this difference in a former paragraph; it may be
enough to repeat here, that while the indefi-

nite past tense of a verb must always be
constructed *as a past*, the perfect, consisting
of the auxiliary "have" with the past participle of the verb, denotes present possession
of the state or act described by that past
participle, and must always be treated and
constructed as a *present*.*

Use of the present to signify fixed design.

257. One more point noticed by my Censor
may serve for our instruction. I had begun
a sentence, "The next point which I notice,
shall be . . ." This he designates as
"confusing the present and the future."
Here again is a mistake as to the usage of
the tenses. There is a very common use of
the present, which has regard, not to actual
time of occurrence, but to *design*. "Do you
go abroad this year?" "I will come unto
you when I shall pass through Macedonia,
for I do pass through Macedonia," 1 Cor.
xvi. 5. In this sense the present was used
in the sentence complained of. "The next
point which I notice," means, "the next
point coming under notice," "the next point
which I mean to notice in my lecture." It
is necessary for one who would write good
grammar, and remark on the grammar of

* See Dr. Latham's "History of the English Language," p. 557.

others, to know the usages of the various tenses, not merely to deal with these tenses as they appear at first sight.

258. "I mention it, because it may be that of many others besides him." This is objected to by one who fills it up thus : " it may be a difficulty of many other people, *besides being a difficulty of him.*" But surely a moment's thought will convince any of us, that such a filling up, nay, that any filling up at all, is quite wrong, and beside the purpose. The pronoun " *him* " is governed by the pre-position, or transitive adverb "*besides.*" "Others besides him " is a clause perfect in itself, and needs no filling up what-ever.

Sentences wrongly supposed elliptic.

259. And this may serve as a caution to us against rashness in this matter of filling up sentences, having hastily assumed them to be elliptical. One of my critics says, "We hear clergymen sometimes say . . . than *him*, than *her*, than *them!* Only place the *verb* after such words—place the words *is* and *are*—and see what nonsense it makes—than *him is*, than *her is*, than *them are.*"

Caution against rash and positive assertions about con-struction.

260. Here is an instance of that against which I would caution my readers. This writer first assumes that the construction of

the phrase is as he wants it to be, and then reasons on his own assumption to prove that the phrase is wrongly expressed. The fact is, that the construction in this case does not admit of any such filling up. I have shown (in paragraph 243), by the unquestioned and unavoidable use of " *than whom,*" that *than* governs an accusative case directly, without any ellipsis whatever. That the other construction, " than he is," is an admissible one, cannot in the slightest degree affect the question whether *this one* is admissible or not. Yet I doubt not that many readers of this illogical critique would be deceived by its rash and positive character, and imagine the point in question to be proved.

'construct" and "construe."

261. "What do you wish us to understand by readers ' *constructing* ' the sentence ? Writers ' *construct :*' readers ' *construe.*' " This is said in reference to my having written that we ought not " to mislead the reader by introducing the possibility of *constructing the sentence* otherwise than as the writer intended." And the objection is instructive, as leading to the indication of the exact meaning and difference of the two words. Suppose I am examining a class of boys, and, with reference to a given sentence,

direct one of them to *construe* the sentence. He knows perfectly well what I mean. He turns the sentence into English, if it be in any other language. But suppose I tell him to *construct* the sentence. He knows, or ought to know, that I mean that he is to explain the construction of the sentence, to give an account of its concords and governments. My Censor's mistake here is, that he transfers the meaning of the verb "*construct*," when applied to building up what did not before exist, to the case of a sentence given as already existing. The word "*construing*," in the sentence quoted, would make sense, and convey a certain meaning not very far removed from that which I intended : but it would not convey that meaning itself, that of supplying a construction—building up the sentence with reference to its concords and governments.

262. A correspondent says, "You make "above. use of the adverb '*above*' as an adjective. Can you use the correlative word '*below*' in the same sense ?" The usage complained of, "the above," meaning something which has been before spoken of, is certainly not elegant, though it is not uncommon. It may easily be avoided, by merely filling

in the ellipsis, and saying "the above-mentioned."

Adjectives used as adverbs.

263. I must say something on the question of adjectives used as adverbs : or rather of the allowable forms of qualifying verbs. The common rule, believed in and universally applied by the ordinary teachers of grammar, is, that we must always qualify a verb by the adverbial form, and never by the adjectival. According to these teachers, such expressions as the following are wrong, " The string of his tongue was loosed, and he spake *plain.*" "The moon shines *bright.*" " How *sweet* the moonlight sleeps upon this bank." "Breathe *soft,* ye winds, ye waters gently flow."

264. These, we are told, ought to have been written with " *plainly,*" " *brightly,*" " *sweetly,*" and " *softly.*" But this is a case where the English language and the common grammarians are at variance. The sentences which I have quoted are but a few out of countless instances in our best writers, and in the most chaste and beautiful passages of our best writers, in which the usage occurs. On examining into it, we find that it is very much matter of arbitrary custom. Some adjectives will bear being thus used : others

will not. Most of those which can be so used seem to be of one syllable ; *plain, soft, sweet, right, wrong,* and the like. In all these cases it may be more precise and accurate to say *plainly, softly, sweetly, rightly, wrongly,* &c., but we certainly can, and our best writers certainly do, use these and other monosyllabic adjectives as adverbs. Still, as far as my memory serves me, they do not often thus use adjectives of more than one syllable. We may say, *He spake plain :* but we cannot so well say " He spoke *simple*," or " He spoke *delightful*." We may say, " The moon shines *bright*," but we can hardly say, " The moon shines brilliant." What may be the reason for this, I do not pretend to say; I only state what seems to be the fact.

265. One of my correspondents tries to make all easy, by suggesting that this adverbial use of adjectives is entirely poetical, and ought never to be allowed in prose. But, begging his pardon, this is assuming the whole question. We undoubtedly *have* the usage in prose, and have it abundantly ; and this being so, to lay down a rule that it cannot be allowed in prose, is to prejudge the matter in dispute.

266. An important consideration may be Two uses of adverbial.

qualifica-
tions,—

introduced into this matter, which has not, I
think, yet been brought to bear on it. There
may be two uses of an adverb as qualifying a
verb. One of these may have respect to the
action indicated by the verb, describing its
mode of performance ; the other may have respect to the result of that action, irrespective
of its mode of performance. We may, if we will,
designate these two uses respectively the subjective and the objective use. And it is to
the latter of them that I would now draw
the reader's attention.

subjective
and ob-
jective.

267. When the adverbial term by which a
verb is qualified is *objectively* used, has respect to the result, and not to the mode, of
acting, there seems no reason why it should
not be an adjective. Take the following :
"Shall not the Judge of all the earth do *right ?*"
Now in these last words, "*do right*," we may
take *right* either as an adverb, "do rightly,"
or as an adjective, "*do that which is right*,"
"*do justice.*" In this particular case, it does
not appear which of the two is intended.
But take another, Neh. ix. 33—"Thou hast
done *right*, but we have done wickedly."
Here it seems almost certain, from the
parallelism, that *right* is meant to be used
adverbially.

268. Now pass on to the other cases in which the adjective is used. " He spake plain." "That which he spake was *plain*." "He spake (that which was) *plain*." Here again it is immaterial to the logical sense whether we take adjective or adverb. "They love him that speaketh right," Prov. xvi. 13. And from these let us advance yet further to those cases where the adjectival sense is not so plainly applicable, but still may be in the thoughts. " The moon shines bright." Here it is plain, that the qualifying word *bright* refers not so much to the mode in which the moon performs her function of shining, as to the result or product of that shining : it is rather objective than subjective. "The moon is giving light, and that light is bright." "Breathe soft " is just as easily understood, " Breathe that which is soft," as " Breathe softly."

269. This after all seems to be the logical account of the usage : and by the rules of thought, not by the dicta of the ordinary grammarians, must all such usages be ultimately judged.

270. The account above given will at once enable us to convict of error such expressions as " looking sadly," " smelling sweetly,"

"looking sadly," &c.

"feeling queerly." For in all these we do not mean to qualify the mode of acting or being, but to describe the result produced by the act or state. To "smell sweetly" is not meant to describe some sweet way of performing the act of smelling, but is meant to describe that the smell itself is sweet. And in this case the verb is of that class called neuter-substantive, *i. e.*, neuter, and akin in construction to the verb substantive "*to be.*" "*The rose smells sweet,*" is in construction much the same as "*the rose is sweet.*" "*You look sad*" is equivalent to "*you seem to be sad.*" And so of the rest.

"it would read oddly."

271. Speaking of an expression which was the subject of remark in one of my lectures, I said, "*it would read rather oddly.*" This was objected to as a violation of the rule above-mentioned. It was not really so. I here used the word "read" in an unusual sense, but at the same time one fully sanctioned by usage : in the sense of "affect the hearer when read." So that it is not a strict neuter-substantive, but a word anomalously used, and used in such a sense as to require the adverb rather than the adjective.

Usage in comparative and super-

272. What has been said hitherto applies to the positive degree of comparison only ; when

we pass beyond that to the comparative and ^{lative} superlative, another consideration comes in. All adverbs do not admit of degrees of comparison. That many do, is acknowledged. *Oftener, oftenest, seldomer,* seem to be good English words. But these exceptions are rare. We cannot say *simplier, brightlier, plainlier.* And in consequence, when we want to express comparative and superlative degrees of qualification of a verb, we commonly have recourse to one of two other constructions : we either take the resolved comparative and superlative, *more plainly, most plainly,* or we take the comparative and superlative of the corresponding adjective. Thus, for instance, we have " *well* " as the adverb of good : we cannot say " *weller* " and " *wellest :* " we do not say " *more well* " and " *most well :* " but we go back to the adjective, and we say, for our comparative and superlative adverbs, *better* and *best.* So, too, whereas we may, in the positive degree, say either "the moon shines *bright,*" or "the moon shines *brightly,*" we should say, in the comparative and superlative, not "the sun shines *more brightly,* and the fire shines *most brightly,*" but, "the sun shines *brighter,* and the fire shines *brightest.*" Take another example. When I wrote (see below, paragraph 380) : "If with your inferiors, speak no *coarser* than usual ; if with your superiors, no *finer ;*" my language was characterised as being ungrammatical, because we cannot say "*to speak coarse.*" True : but, as we have seen, what cannot be done in the positive, must be done in the other degrees of comparison : and my sentence was strictly correct, and according to usage. In this case too, there was no choice open between the two forms, the resolved and the adjectival comparative. Had I written, "speak no more coarsely," "speak no more finely," the conjunction of "speak" with "no more" would have been awkward, as suggesting a temporal meaning which was foreign (see paragraph 301) to the construction of the sentence. And had I adopted the form of expression which my Censor recommends, "speak not more coarsely than usual," I might have escaped indeed his censure, but not the charge of having written pompous and pedantic English.

'a decided weak point.'

273. Exception is taken to an expression occurring in these notes, "a decided weak point." But there can be no doubt that my Censor is wrong. A "*decidedly weak point*" is one thing; a "*decided weak point*" is another. There is a difference, according as we regard

the adverb as qualifying only the adjective, or the adjective and substantive together. "There occurs in his book a remarkable prefatory announcement." Who would think of saying "a *remarkably* prefatory announcement?" Thus also in the phrase under consideration, had I written "a *decidedly* weak point, I should have spoken of *a point decidedly weak;* but writing as I did a *decided* weak point, I spoke of a *weak point of whose existence there could be no doubt.*

274. If we use our powers of observation, Anomalies. we shall find in the usage of adjectives and adverbs, as in other usages, many things which follow no rule but that of custom, and of which it is very difficult to give any reasonable account. I mention this to show how inadequate the laws of ordinary grammar are to regulate or even to describe our practice.

275. Take but one example out of many; "long" and the use of the adjectives *long* and *short*, with "short." reference to adverbial construction. *Long* is an adverb as well as an adjective. We say "How long," speaking of time. "Paul was long speaking." We have no adverb "*longly*," though we have "*widely*," "*broadly*," "*deeply*." Now observe the adjective "*short*." Its use as an adverb is hardly legitimate. Your

banker asks you whether you will *take it short*, when you present a cheque to be cashed; but this use is a technical one. But what I wish to observe is, that the adverb "*shortly*" is by our usage limited to one department only of the meanings of the adjective, viz., that of *time;* and in that department, to time future. We cannot use *shortly* of time past; we cannot use it of duration—"*he preached shortly;*" but we must use it of that which is to come, "I hope *shortly* to see you."

"just now." 276. This mention of adverbs of time reminds me of an expression which usage has assigned to time past, as it has that other to time future. "*Just now*," in its strict meaning, imports, nearly at the present moment, whether before or after. Yet our general usage has limited its application to a point slightly preceding the present, and will not allow us to apply it to that which is to come. If we are asked "When?" and we reply "Just now," we are understood to describe an event past, not an event future.

277. In this case we have the double use of the term preserved in provincial usage. In the midland and northern counties we have such a sentence as "I'll be with you just now," which is perfectly right in logical

precision, though proscribed by English usage.

278. The use of the indicative and sub-junctive moods, after conditional particles, as *if* and *whether*, is a wide subject, and one on which considerable uncertainty seems to prevail. The general rule appears plain enough : that when matter of *fact* is concerned, we should use the indicative : when matter of doubt, the subjunctive. "Whether I *be* master or you, one thing is plain." Here we have doubt : it is left in uncertainty which of the two is master. "You shall soon see whether I *am* master, or you." Here there is no uncertainty : your eyes shall see and be enlightened as to a fact, of which the speaker at all events has no doubt. *Subjunctive and indicative moods in conditional sentences.*

The general rule.

279. The same rule has been thus clearly laid down by Dr. Latham : "The following method of determining the amount of doubt expressed in a conditional proposition is useful : insert, immediately after the conjunction, one of the two following phrases : (1) *as is the case;* (2) *as may or may not be the case.* By ascertaining which of these two supplements expresses the meaning of the speaker, we ascertain the mood of the verb which follows. When the first formula is the one required, *Stated by Dr Latham.*

there is no element of doubt, and the verb should be in the indicative mood. *If (as is the case) he is gone, I must follow him.* When the second formula is the one required, there *is* an element of doubt, and the verb should be in the subjunctive mood. *If (as may or may not be the case) he be gone, I must follow him.**

Ignorance of this rule.

280. When a correspondent said of the first sentence in my second lecture, "If a man values his peace of mind, let him not write on the Queen's English," that I ought to have written "If a man value his peace of mind," he apparently was in ignorance of this very plain rule. For that every man does value his peace of mind, is of course assumed, and the phrase to be supplied is the former one in Dr. Latham's rule. "If *(as is the case)* a man values his peace of mind."

This rule perhaps unknown to our older writers.

281. But this rule, satisfactory as it is for a guide, does not seem to have been known to our older writers. Our translators of the Bible notoriously do not observe it. In cases where the original (and the rule is not one belonging to English only, but to the conditions of thought) has the indicative, and the

* *History of the English Language,* p. 646.

missing phrase clearly must be, "*as is the case,*" they have used the subjunctive. An instance of this is found in Col. iii. 1, " If ye then *be* risen with Christ . . . ; " which according to the original ought to be " If ye then *are* risen." The fact, that those addressed are thus risen, is proved in the previous chapter, and the Apostle proceeds to ground upon it the exhortations that follow. " If (*as is the case ;* as I have proved) ye are risen with Christ." Many more instances might be given to shew, that our translators almost universally used the subjunctive mood after conditional particles, where we should now use the indicative.

282. Sometimes they seem to use the two moods indifferently. An example is found in Job xxxi. 5—10. "If I have walked with vanity, or my foot *hath hasted* to deceit: let me," &c. " If my step *hath turned* out of the way, and my heart walked after mine eyes, and if any blot *hath cleaved* to mine hands ; then let me," &c. So far is indicative. But Job goes on in the same strain, and our translators in the next place adopt the subjunctive " If mine heart *have been* deceived by a woman . . . . then let," &c.

283. In some places, they seem to have

observed the rule. "If now thou hast understanding, hear this."—Job xxxiv. 16.

284. The same irregularity appears to
prevail in their construction of verbs after
"though." Take as an example Col. ii. 5 :
"Though I be absent in the flesh." Here
the Apostle is asserting his absence as a fact,
and the Greek verb is in the indicative, as
by the ordinary rule the English should be
also : "Though (as is the fact) I am absent
in the flesh."

Bias form r-
ly to the
subjunctiv.

285. I believe it will be found, on the
whole, that there is a decided bias on the
part of our translators to the use of the subjunctive mood. I do not of course speak of
the use of "be" as an indicative, as in
2 Kings ix. 9 : "Ye be righteous." This
sometimes brings in ambiguity as to which
mood is actually used in a conditional sentence : as in Gen. xlii. 19, "If ye be true
men." But I speak of the prevalence of the
use of undoubted subjunctives, determined to
be so by the auxiliary, or by the form of the
verb itself.

but more to
the indica-
tive.

286. But if there was a bias then in favour
of the subjunctive, the bias is as decidedly
now against it. Our conditional sentences in
common talk are almost all expressed in the

indicative. "I don't know whether I shall be at the committee; but if I *am,* I will mention it." This every one says. "If I *be,*" would sound pedantic. We all say, "whether it is, or not, I cannot say:" not "whether it be." And so of other conditional sentences.

287. Here then we seem to have a pheno- menon, instructive to those who are more anxious to watch the actually flowing currents of verbal usage, than to build up bounds for them to run in. We have a well known logical rule, prevailing in our own and in other languages, and laid down by gram- marians as to be followed. But it would seem that it never has been followed univer- sally: that it has not regulated the language of the Book in commonest use, and yet that the language of that book speaks intelligibly to us. And more than this: for while that book violates the rule almost uniformly in one direction, we ourselves as uniformly violate it in the other.

Phenome- non to be observed.

288. While speaking upon the indicative and subjunctive moods, I may notice that the use of the bare verb without "*may,*" or "*might,*" or "*should,*" after the conjunction "*that,*" which we not unfrequently meet with in the English version of the Bible, and

Verb after "that" without an auxiliary.

in the Common Prayer-book, is not ungrammatical, nor is it to be corrected by inserting the apparently missing auxiliary verb, as I have heard some clergymen do in reading. The verb thus used was the old form of the subjunctive, now generally supplanted by the resolved form with the auxiliary. Thus when we pray "that our hearts may be unfeignedly thankful, and that we shew forth thy praise not only with our lips but in our lives," the verb "*shew*" is as truly in the subjunctive as the verb "*be*" in "that I be not ashamed," or the verb "*slip*" in "hold thou up my goings in thy paths, that my footsteps slip not." That this is so, is conclusively shown by consulting the older versions. In John xv. 2, for example, "he purgeth it, that it may bring forth more fruit," is, in Wiclif's version, "he shall purge it that it bere the more fruyt." In ver. 16, "that whatsoever ye shall ask of the Father in my name, he may give it you," is "that whatever things ye axen the fadir in my name, he give to you :" and so on, wherever the auxiliary is found in the more modern version.

Singulars and Plurals.

289. We will now pass on to another matter—the use of *singulars* and *plurals.* It is a general rule, that when a verb has

two or more nominative cases to which it belongs, it must be in the plural number. But let us take care what we mean by this in each case. When I say "John and James are here," I mean "John is here, and James is here;" "but when I say, "*the evening and the morning were the first day,*" I do not mean "the evening was the first day, and the morning was the first day," but I mean "*the evening and the morning together made up the first day.*" So that here is an important difference. I may use a plural verb when it is true of both its nouns separately, and also when it is only true of them taken together. Now how is this in another example? Am I to say "*two and two are four,*" or "*two and two is four?*" Clearly I cannot say *are* in the first explanation, for it cannot be true that two is four and two is four. But how on the second? Here as clearly I may be grammatically correct in saying "two and two are four," if, that is, I understand something for the two and the four to apply to: two apples and two apples make (*are*) four apples. But when I assert the thing merely as an arithmetical truth, *with no apples*, I do not see how "*are*" can be right. I am saying that the sum of two numbers, which I express by *two and two*, *is*, makes up, another number, *four;* and in all abstract cases, where we merely speak of numbers, the verb is better singular : two and two *"is"* four, not *"are."*

"twice one are two."

290. The last case was a somewhat doubtful one. But the following, arising out of it, is not so :—We sometimes hear children made to say, "twice one *are* two." For this there is no justification whatever. It is a plain violation of the first rules of grammar ; " *twice one* " not being plural at all, but *strictly singular.* Similarly, "three times three *are* nine " is clearly wrong, and so are all such expressions; what we want to say being simply this, that three taken three times makes up, *is* equal to nine. You may as well say, " nine are three times three," as " three times three are nine."

Cases not understood.

291. There still are cases in which those who do not think about the composition of a sentence may find a difficulty as to whether a singular or a plural verb should follow two nouns coupled together by " *and*." The difficulty arises from the fact that " *and*" has many meanings. Sometimes it imports addition: sometimes it merely denotes an apposition, or simultaneous predication of two characters or qualities belonging to one and

the same thing. And it is in this latter case that a difficulty arises, and a mistake is often made. Take, for instance, this sentence, where the writer is speaking of the cheapness of Bibles at the present day: "The only revelation of God's will to mankind, and the only record of God's dealings with men, is now to be obtained for a sum which a labouring man might save out of one day's wages." Now what is meant by this sentence is, "That book, which is the only revelation of God's will to men, and at the same time the only record of God's dealings with men, is now to be obtained," &c. One thing, and not two, is the subject of the sentence. Yet in a precisely similar sentence of my own the other day, the people at the printing-office, more studious for the letter of grammar, than for the spirit of thought, corrected *is* into *are*. And observe the effect on the meaning. If I say, "The only revelation of God's will to men, and the only record of God's dealings with men, *are* to be obtained," &c., I convey the idea that I am speaking of two books, one containing the only revelation of God's will, the other, the only record of his dealings. It is obvious that the writer might have cast the sentence into another form, and having said that the

Bible contains the only revelation of God's will, and the only record of God's dealings, might have gone on to say, "Both these are to be obtained," &c.; but constructed as the sentence now is, the singular verb, and not the plural, is required to express his meaning.

292. Take another case.   In Psalm xiv. 7, we read, " Destruction and unhappiness *is* in their ways:" in Psalm lxxiii. 25, "My flesh and my heart *faileth.*"   Again, as was remarked by the critic in the "Times" of September 29th, 1863, in censuring the modernizations in the Cambridge Shakspeare, Shakspeare wrote "His steeds to water at those springs on chaliced flowers that *lies:*" and Prospero is made to say, "*lies* at my mercy all mine enemies."   How are these apparent violations of grammar to be accounted for?

293. Simply, I believe, by regarding the sense of the sentences.   In each of them, one and the same act is predicated of a number of persons or things, considered as one. In the two former sentences, these things are nearly synonymous: in the two latter, they are classed together.   In either case, the act is one: and this fact seems to have ruled the verb in the singular, instead of the more usual plural.   It has been mentioned before

Account of these usages.

in these notes, that in the Greek language a plural of the neuter gender takes after it a singular verb. The things composing it are considered as forming one mass rather than a plurality of individuals, and the verb is ruled accordingly.

294. Care is required in the use of several conjunctional and prepositional particles. The first of these which I shall notice is "*except.*" *Except* means *with the exception of :* and exempts from some previous list, or some previous predication, the substantive or substantives, or clause or clauses, before which it is placed. "*All were pleased, except Juno :*" i.e., "*with the exception of Juno,*" or, "*Juno being excepted.*" And on this account, we must take care that the person or thing excepted be one which would have been included in the previous category, if the exception had not been made.

Use of certain conjunctional particles.

295. This rule is violated in the following sentence taken from a newspaper : "Few ladies, except Her Majesty, could have made themselves heard," &c. For how is the word "except" here to be understood ? From what list is Her Majesty excepted, or taken out ? Clearly not from among the *few ladies* spoken of. Had the sentence stood "All

Violation of this rule.

ladies, except Her Majesty, would have proved unequal to," &c., it would have been constructed rightly, though clumsily; what it meant to express was that "Few ladies *besides* Her Majesty, could have" done what was spoken of: and "*besides*" should have been the word used. *Besides* (by the side of) does not *subtract*, as *except* does, but *adds;* and thus we should have the sense required: viz., that very few ladies *added to* Her Majesty,—*besides* her,—could have done the thing spoken of.

Use of "except" for "unless."

296. There is a use of *except*, which was once very common, but is now hardly ever found: that, I mean, by which it stands for "*unless.*" "I will not let thee go, except thou bless me." This usage is quite legitimate: amounting in fact to saying, "In no case will I let thee go, excepted only that in which thou shalt bless me." This is found constantly throughout the English version of the Bible, both in the Old Testament and in the New.

"without."

297. *Without* is another word used in somewhat the same meaning. As in the other cases, its prepositional use has led to its conjunctional. Take the following sentence from Sir Philip Sidney: "You will never live to my age, without you keep yourselves in breath

with exercise, and in heart with joyfulness."
In this, "*without you keep*" is in fact a construction compounded of "*without keeping*,"
and "*unless*" or "*except you keep*."

298. What are we to think of the expression, "*a mutual friend ?*" What is "*mutual ?*"
Much the same as "*reciprocal*." It describes
that which passes from each to each of two
persons. Thus for example, when St. Paul
says to the Romans (i. 12), "That I may be
comforted together with you by the mutual
faith both of you and me," the meaning is, in
English, "by my confidence in you and your
confidence in me." And that our translators
meant this to be understood is clear : for
they deliberately altered the previous versions
to this form. Wiclif had "bi faith that is
bothe youre and myn to gidre :" Tyndall,
"through the common faith which bothe ye
and I have :" so also Cranmer and the Geneva
Bible.

"a mutual friend."

299. And *mutual* ought never to be used,
unless the reciprocity exists. "The *mutual
love* of husband and wife " is correct enough :
but "a *mutual friend* of both husband and
wife" is sheer nonsense. A *common* friend
is meant ; a friend that is common to both.
The word *mutual* has no place or assignable

meaning in such a phrase, and yet we occasionally find it used even by those who pride themselves on correct speaking.

" we will write you." 300. There is an expression frequently used in correspondence, principally by mercantile men : "we will *write you*," instead of " we will *write to you :*" "*write me* at your earliest convenience," instead of " *write to me.*" Is this an allowable ellipsis ? It is universally acknowledged that the "to" of the so-called dative case may be dropped in certain constructions : "He did me a favour ;" "He sent me a birthday present ;" "He wrote me a kind letter :" "The Lord raised them up deliverers." In all these cases, the object or act which the verb directly governs is expressed. But if it be omitted, the verb at once is taken as governing the personal pronoun or substantive, of which the dative case is thus elliptically expressed. Thus : "He sent me " would mean, not "He sent to me," but *he sent*, as his messenger, *me*. "The Lord raised them up," would imply, not that He raised up some person or thing *for them*, but that He lifted them up themselves.

301. And so, when we drop the substantive directly governed by the verb in the phrase

" He wrote me a letter," or "he wrote me word," and merely say "he *wrote me,*" we cannot properly understand the sentence in any other way, than that "*me*" is governed by the verb "*wrote.*" That this is nonsense, is not to the purpose. The construction of such a phrase necessarily halts, and is defective, not only elliptical. We should say in all cases, "*write to me,*" or "*write me word,*" or the like ; never barely "write me."

302. Very curious blunders in construction are made by the careless use of "*and*" with the *relative pronoun,* coupling it to a sentence which will not bear such coupling. I take these two instances from one and the same page of a charitable report : "The Board offer their grateful acknowledgments for the liberal support hitherto so freely extended, *and which* has so greatly contributed to this satisfactory result." "It was feared that the untimely death of the surgeon to the hospital, occurring as it did so very shortly after its opening, *and to whose* untiring energy the Institution mainly owes its existence, might seriously affect its future prospects and position."

303. Now in both these instances the conjunction "*and*" is wholly unneeded, is indeed

" and which."

9

quite in the way of the construction. Two clauses connected by "and" must be similarly constructed. You cannot say, "Then I went home and which is quite true." Yet this is the construction of both the sentences quoted: and the fault is one of the very commonest in the writing of careless or half-educated persons.

304. In the *Times* of this very day, Nov. 11, 1863, I find the following sentence, occurring in the translation of M. Casimir Perrier's letter to the President of the Legislative body : "I hoped to procure the original placard which was posted on the walls of Grenoble on that occasion, *but which* I have been unable to do."

The following "Form of Order" is distributed widely by a London publisher :—
"*Please send me a copy of the* SHAKESPEARE MEMORIAL, and for which *I enclose Eighteen Postage Stamps.*" I was surprised to find, that Murray's Handbooks for Italy *abound* with this vulgarism.

"one" joined to "his."

305. There is an unfortunate word in our language, which few can use without very soon going wrong in grammar, or, which is worse, in common sense. It is the word "*one*," used in the sense of the French "*on*," or the

German, " *man*," and meaning people in general.

> " What one has done, when one was young,
>   One ne'er will do again ;
> In former days one went by coach,
>   But now one goes by train."

So far, " *one* " is pretty sure to be right. It is only when this is carried on further, that the danger arises. Suppose I wanted to put into English the saying of the French gourmand, which, by the way, I am glad an Englishman did not originally utter : " Avec cette sauce on pourrait manger son propre père ; "—how am I to express myself ? In other words, how am I to take up the " *one* " with the possessive pronoun, or with any possessive, in English ? The French, we see, say, " With this sauce one could eat his own father." Is this an English usage (I don't mean the meal, but the grammar) ? I believe not, though it is becoming widely spread in current literature.

> " In such a scene one might forget his cares,
>   And dream himself, in poet's mood, away."

And one of my correspondents says, " When writing on language, grammar, and composition, *one* ought to be more than usually particular in *his* endeavours to be *himself* correct."

These sentences do not seem to me to be right. Having used "*one*," we must also use "*one's*" cares, and "*one's*" self. We must say, at the risk of sacrificing elegance of sound,

> "In such a scene one might forget one's cares,
>   And dream one's self, in poet's mood, away."

The fact is, that this "*one*" is a very awkward word to get into a long sentence. I have sometimes seen it in our newspapers, followed not only by "*he*" and "*his*," but by "*they*" and "*their*," and "*we*" and "*our*," in all stages of happy confusion.

"didn't use," "hadn't used," &c.

306. There is another word in our common English very difficult to keep right. It is the verb "*use*," signifying to be accustomed. "I *used* to meet him at my uncle's." When the verb is affirmatively put in this manner, there is no difficulty, and no chance of going wrong. These arise when we want to put it in the negative; to speak of something which we were not accustomed to do. And then we find rather curious combinations. I "*didn't use*," I "*hadn't used*," I "*wasn't used*." This latter would be legitimate

enough, if the verb were "*used to,*" meaning "*accustomed by use to.*" We may say, "*I wasn't used to the practice.*" But it will be plain that it is a different meaning of which I am now speaking. A friend tells me that in his part of the world the people say, "didn't use to was :" and a midland correspondent, that he has heard in his town, even in good society, the phrase, "*used to could.*"

307. If you ask me what we are to say in this case, I must reply that I can answer very well on paper, but not so well for the purposes of common talk. "*I used*" is negatived by "*I used not.*" But unfortunately, this expression does not do the work in common talk. "*I used not to see him at my uncle's,*" does not convey the idea that it was not your habit to meet him there. It rather means, that he was there, but that for some unexplained reason you did not see him. You meant to express, not something which it *was* your practice *not to do*, but something which it *was not* your practice *to do.* "*I never used*" is better, but it may be too strong. I am afraid there is no refuge but in the inelegant word "*usedn't,*" to which I suppose most of us have many times been driven.

"riding" or
"driving."

308. *Riding* or *driving?* This question has been asked by several correspondents, in consequence of my story, told further on, of a benevolent old gentleman *"riding in his carriage."* I am asked whether this ought not to have been *"driving,"* seeing that riding cannot properly be predicated except of persons on horseback. But there is not necessarily any such limitation of the meaning of the word to *ride.* It comes certainly from a time when the employment of wheels was almost unknown: but from centuries ago has been applied to any kind of locomotion in which a person or thing is borne, whether on an animal, or in a carriage, or as when used of a ship on the water. A *road* is a broad path on which people may *ride* on horses and in vehicles: a *road,* or *rade,* for ships, is a part of the sea where they may *ride,* or be borne at anchor. We have in Jer. xvii. 25, "Riding in chariots and on horses:" and such, as may be seen in the dictionaries, is the usage of all English writers.

"I take it.

309. It is a curious symptom of our having forgotten the usages of the best age of English, that several correspondents should have objected to my having written *" I take*

it," signifying, "such is my opinion." For it is constantly found, from Shakspeare onwards, in this sense : and the sense is amply justified by other cognate usages of the verb to take : such as, *to take it well or ill, to take it in good part, to take a man for his brother,* and the like. The fact of such an objection having been made, shows the necessity for upholding our plain nervous colloquial English against the inroads of modern fine language. It would be a loss instead of a gain if "*I take it,*" were to be superseded by "*I apprehend ;*" or, as we should be sure to have it pronounced, "*I happryend.*"

310. Another correspondent inquires respecting the construction of such sentences as the following :—"Day and night are a consequence of the earth revolving on its axis." He maintains, that here, *revolving* is a verbal noun equivalent to *revolution,* and that we ought to say, "A consequence of the *earth's revolving* on its axis." He believes that he has proved this by the test of substituting the pronoun for the earth, thus : "Day and night on our earth are a consequence of *its revolving* on its axis," where he rightly says no one would think of saying *it revolving.*

311. At first sight this appears decisive.

"the earth's revolving."

But let us examine a little further. It is somewhat curious that, in this last sentence, we may leave out the possessive pronoun, without obscuring the sense. "Our earth enjoys day and night as a consequence of revolving on its axis." To which a rejoinder may be made, "of *what* revolving on its axis?" and the answer is "*the earth*," not "*the earth's*." We may, if we wish, regard *the earth revolving on its axis* as a description of an idea set before the mind. The fact indicated by that idea, viz., that the earth does so revolve, produces as a consequence day and night. Day and night, in other words, are a consequence of that fact so indicated : *i.e.*, of the *earth revolving* on her axis.

312. I believe, then, that both forms are correct in point of construction : and a writer will use one or the other, according as euphony admits or requires. In an instance which my correspondent cited from my first paper, where I say that "the profusion of commas prevented the text being understood," it is plain that "the text's being understood" would have been harsh and ill-sounding. I believe that, as a general matter of choice, I rather prefer the form of the sentence to which my correspondent objects. It may be

that my ears are accustomed to the Greek and Latin construction, which is according to this form and not to the other.

313. A correspondent finds that the newspapers are in the habit of using "*predicate*" where they mean "*predict.*" I have not observed this ; but it may be well to say, that to *predicate* is simply to affirm this or that of anything, whereas to *predict* is to foretell a future event.

"predicate" for "predict."

314. There are certain cases where either word might be used without a fault. And such is the very instance cited by my correspondent :—"It is impossible to predicate what the result will be." The writer very likely meant, to *predict;* but he might have intended to say, that no one can *predicate* this or that probable result. If so, he expressed himself clumsily, but did not fall into the error complained of.

315. "*If*" for "*whether,*" is another mistake which I am asked to point out. But this usage, though it may not be according to our modern habit, is found in our best writers ; and I cannot see that there is anything to complain of in it. Under the word "*if,*" in Johnson, we have, cited from Dryden :

"if" for "whether."

" Uncertain if by augury or chance."

And from Prior,

> " doubting if she doubts or no."

We also read (Gen. viii. 8) that Noah "sent forth a dove from him, to see if the waters were abated from off the face of the ground."

"seldom or never."

316. Another of my correspondents is offended with "*seldom or never*," and prefers "*seldom, if ever*." It seems to me that the two express the same idea in slightly differing ways, but that both are perfectly legitimate. The one is analogous to "*very little, or not at all*," the other to "*very little, if at all*."

"like I do."

317. "*Like*," used as an adverb, is also brought under my notice, and the complaint in this case is not without reason. "*Like I do now*," "*like he was*," "*like we are*," are quite indefensible, and are avoided by all careful speakers and writers. The mistake has been occasioned by the legitimate use of "*like*" as an adjective at the beginning of a sentence, where it means "*like to*." You may say, "*Like David*, I am the youngest of my family :" but you may not say, "*Like David was*, I am the youngest of my family.*"

Nouns of number.

318. *Nouns of number* are also proposed as a subject for treatment. I am supposed to have written incorrectly "When the band of

French Guides were in this country;" and the opinion is supported by reminding me that we say "There was a large congregation," not "there were a large congregation." Most true : and from the consideration of this example we may derive something like a rule in such cases. In saying "*there was a large congregation,*" I am speaking of the assembly *as a whole.* If I were saying anything which suggested the idea of the *individuals composing it,* I should use, not the singular verb, but the plural. I should hardly say, "*the congregation was not all of the same opinion,*" but "*the congregation were not all of the same opinion.*" The slightest bias either way will influence a writer, when using such words, towards a singular or a plural verb. I should say, that in the case complained of, perhaps it was the fact of "*Guides,*" in the plural, being the word immediately preceding the verb, that induced me to put it in the plural ; or perhaps the knowledge that I was about to speak of the band throughout the following sentences, as "*they,*" "*the Frenchmen,*" &c.

318*a.* "*People*" and "*persons.*" A correspondent wishes me to observe, that the former of these terms signifies an aggregate of *persons,*

"People" and "persons."

and that we ought never to say *several people*, but always *several persons*. I own I cannot find that this distinction is entirely borne out. Bacon, as adduced by Johnson, says, "If a man temper his actions so as to content *every combination of people*, the musick will be the fuller :" in which sentence, "*people*" seems to be used for "*persons*." Still, it is a distinction which it is worth while to remember : for doubtless it is so far just, that it represents the general import of the two words.

"I know nothing by myself," explained.
319. Another correspondent is puzzled by my having said that " a man who talks of Aristobŭlus in the lesson, is as likely as not to preach from St. Paul's, '*I know nothing by myself*,' to show us that the apostle *wanted divine teaching*, and not to be aware that he meant he *was not conscious of any fault*." My correspondent cannot conceive how the words can have any other meaning, than that the apostle had no knowledge of his own. His difficulty (and I mention it because it may be that of many others besides him) is that he has missed the peculiar sense of the preposition "*by*," as here used. It bears the sense of "*of*," in the words "*I know no harm of him*." This is still in the midland counties, "*I know no harm by him*." We have a somewhat

similar usage in the Prayer-book version of
Ps. xv. 4, "*He that setteth not by himself*," *i. e.*,
is not self-conceited, setteth not store by himself, as we even now say. I have heard a
parish clerk pronounce these last words, "*he
that sitteth not by himself*," in allusion, I suppose, to the Squire's pew. To return to "*I
know nothing by myself.*" The meaning is
decided for us by the original Greek, which is
simply, "I am conscious of no fault :" and if
is plain that the words of the English version
were so understood when they were first
written ; for Dr. Donne, in King James the
First's time, preaches on them, and quotes
them over and over again, in this sense.

320. A correspondent who gives me his "the three
name vouches for the following anecdote. I 'poys' just
own I had fancied it was an old story : but so mentioned.
many things related in Joe Miller have happened again within my own experience, that I
must not too readily admit a doubt of my
correspondent's accuracy. "My friend," he
says, "happened to be present one Sabbath in
a parish church some miles north of Aberdeen,
the clergyman of which (a true Gael) read to
his hearers a portion of the book of Daniel,
containing the names 'Shadrach, Meshach,
and Abednego.' The reverend gentleman

finding some difficulty in delivering himself of
these vocables, resolved not to attempt the
task a second time, but simply referred to
'*the three "poys" just mentioned.*'"

I have received another and fuller account
of this kind of abbreviation, certified with the
name of the hearer, which is a guarantee for
its accuracy. In this case the officiating clergyman said, "*same three gentlemen*," and instead of repeating the details of instruments,
"sackbut, psaltery," &c., read, "*music as
before.*"

"religion in
the arm-
chair."   321. In illustration, not of the habit of
mispronouncing, but, what is worse, of mis-
understanding, another correspondent assures
me that he heard a man, pretending to be
a teacher of the Gospel, preach on what he
called "Religion in the arm-chair," his text
being (1 Tim. v. 4), '*Let them learn first to
show piety at home:*' where the word "*piety*,"
as the margin of the English Bible would have
informed him, means merely "*kindness to
their relations*," and has nothing to do with
religion in the stricter sense.

322. A correspondent sends me the following. "A placard is to be seen in a certain
farmyard in this county :—

"'There is a place for everything, and

everything for a place. Any person offending against these rules will forfeit 2d.'"

323. By-the-by, what are we to think of the phrase which came in during the Crimean war, *"The right man in the right place"*? How can the right man ever be in the wrong place? or the wrong man in the right place? We used to illustrate the unfitness of things by saying that the round man had got into the square hole, and the square man into the round hole; that was correct enough; but it was the *putting incongruous things together* that was wrong, not the man, nor the hole. "the right man in the right place."

324. This puts me in mind of the servant at school once coming into the schoolroom, in consequence of some interchange of slippers, and calling out, "Has any gentleman got *his wrong slippers?*" Now, if they were his, they were not wrong; and if they were wrong, they were not his. " his wrong slippers."

325. In the same note, my friend sends me the following: A Mr. Crispin of Oxford announced that he sold "boots and shoes made by celebrated Hoby, London." Mr. Hoby, irate, put into the Oxford paper: "The boots and shoes Mr. Crispin says he sells of my make is a lie."

326. Some odd *descriptions* of men have Ambiguous

descriptions of men. been forwarded me, arising from the ambiguous junction of compound words. In two or three places in London, we see "*Old and New Bookseller*"—an impossible combination in one and the same man; but of course meaning a seller of old and new books. Another tradesman describes himself as "*Gas-holder and Boiler-maker*," meaning that he makes gasholders and boilers, but giving the idea that he undertakes to contain gas himself. We had in Canterbury a worthy neighbour, who advertised himself as "Indigenous Kentish Herbalist;" meaning, of course, not that he was born amongst us, but that he made *herbs indigenous in Kent* his study.

327. I have lying on my table a note just received, in the following words : "R. C. begs to apologise for not acknowledging P. O. order at the time (but was from home), and thus got delayed, misplaced, and forgotten."

A correspondent sends me the following note : "Mrs. A.'s compliments to Mrs. B., and begs to say that C. lived with her for a year and found her respectable, steady, and honest."

"by applying." 328. "*By doing a thing*," for "*if he will do it*," is noticed by a friend as a common error in Scotch papers.

"Found on board the steamer 'Vulcan,' a

gold locket. The owner may have it *by* giving the date, when lost, and paying expenses."

"Found, in Stockwell Street, on Friday early, a gold or gold-plated Geneva watch. The owner may have the same on proving his property, *by* applying to Mr. R. B., 166, Hospital Street."

329. Is it right, a correspondent asks, to say "his hair wants cutting," "the lawn wants mowing?" I should say, undoubtedly. His hair wants a certain act performed on it. What is that process called? *Cutting.* The word is, of course, a present participle, but it is used almost as a substantive. Thus we say, "the first and second mowings of the lawn were difficult, the third was easier." Thus, too, we speak of a "flogging;" of "readings" of Shakspeare, &c. "*He wants his hair cutting*" cannot be similarly defended, nor indeed at all; it ought to be, "he wants his hair *cut.*" "wants cutting."

330. But I now come, from the by-rules and details of the use of the language, to speak of an abuse far more serious than those hitherto spoken of; even the tampering with and deteriorating the language itself. I believe it to have been in connexion with an abuse of this kind, that the term "the King's Deterioration of the language itself.

English" was first devised. We know that it is a crime to clip the King's coin; and the phrase in which we first find the term which forms the subject of our essay, is, "*clipping the King's English.*" So that it is not improbable that the analogy between debasing language and debasing coin first led to it.

Sources of our language.

331. Now in this case the charge is twofold; that of clipping, and that of beating out and thinning down the Queen's English. And it is wonderful how far these, especially the latter, have proceeded in our days. It is well to bear in mind, that our English comes mainly from two sources; rather, perhaps, that its parent stock, the British, has been cut down, and grafted with the two scions which form the present tree:—the Saxon, through our Saxon invaders; and the Latin, through our Norman invaders. Of these two, the Saxon was, of course, the earlier, and it forms the staple of the language. Almost all its older and simpler ideas, both for things and acts, are expressed by Saxon words. But as time went on, new wants arose, new arts were introduced, new ideas needed words to express them; and these were taken from the stores of the classic languages, either direct, or more often through the French. We all

remember that Gurth and Wamba complain, in "Ivanhoe," that the farm-animals, as long as they had the toil of tending them, were called by the Saxon and British names, *ox, sheep, calf, pig;* but when they were cooked and brought to table, their invaders and lords enjoyed them under the Norman and Latin names of *beef, mutton, veal,* and *pork.* This is characteristic enough; but it lets us, in a few words, into an important truth. Even so the language grew; its nerve, and vigour, and honesty, and manliness, and toil, mainly brought down to us in native Saxon terms, while all its vehicles of abstract thought and science, and all its combinations of new requirements as the world went on, were clothed in a Latin garb. To this latter class belong all those larger words in *-ation* and *-atious,* the words compounded with *ex* and *in* and *super,* and the like.

332. It would be mere folly in a man to attempt to confine himself to one or other of these two main branches of the language in his writing or his talk. They are inseparable; welded together, and overlapping each other, in almost every sentence which we use. But short of exclusive use of one or the other, there is a very great difference in respect

of the *amount* of use between writers and speakers. He is ever the most effective writer and speaker, who knows how to build the great body of his discourse out of his native Saxon; availing himself indeed of those other terms without stint, as he needs them, but not letting them give the character and complexion to the whole.

333. Unfortunately, all the tendency of the lower kind of writers of modern English is the other way. The language, as known and read by thousands of Englishmen and Englishwomen, is undergoing a sad and rapid process of deterioration. Its fine manly Saxon is getting diluted into long Latin words not carrying half the meaning. This is mainly owing to the vitiated and pretentious style which passes current in our newspapers. The writers in our journals seem to think that a fact must never be related in print in the same terms in which it would be told by word of mouth. The greatest offenders in this point are the country journals, and, as might be expected, just in proportion to their want of real ability. Next to them comes the London penny press; indeed, it is hardly a whit better; and highest in the scale, but still by no means free from this fault, the

Process of degeneration: whence mainly arising.

regular London press—its articles being for the most part written by men of education and talent in the various political circles. The main offence of the newspapers, the head and front of their offending, is, the insisting on calling common things by uncommon names; changing our ordinary short Saxon nouns and verbs for long words derived from the Latin. And when it is remembered that *In what consisting.* this is very generally done by men for the most part ignorant of the derivation and strict meaning of the words they use, we may imagine what delightful confusion is thus introduced into our language. A Latin word which really has a meaning of its own, and might be a very useful one if confined to that meaning, does duty for some word, whose significance extends far wider than its own meaning; and thereby to common English hearers loses its own proper force, besides utterly confusing their notions about the thing which its new use intended to represent.

334. Our journals seem indeed determined *Dialect of our journals.* to banish our common Saxon words altogether. You never read in them of a *man*, or a *woman*, or a *child*. A man is an "*individual*," or a "*person*," or a "*party*;" a

woman is a *"female;"* or if unmarried, a *"young person,"* which expression, in the newspapers, is always of the feminine gender; a child is a *"juvenile,"* and children *en masse* are expressed by that most odious term, *"the rising generation."* As to the former words, it is certainly curious enough that the same debasing of our language should choose, in order to avoid the good honest Saxon *man,* two words, *"individual"* and *"party,"* one of which expresses a man's *unity,* and the other, in its common untechnical use, belongs to man *associated.* And why should a *woman* be degraded from her position as a rational being, and be expressed by a word which might belong to any animal tribe, and which, in our version of the Bible, is never used except of animals, or of the abstract, the sex in general? Why not call a man a *"male,"* if a woman is to be a *"female"*?

"party." 335. The word *party* for a man is especially offensive. Strange to say, the use is not altogether modern. It occurs in the English version of the apocryphal book of Tobit vi. 7, " If an evil spirit trouble any, one must make a smoke thereof before the man or the woman, and the party shall be no more vexed." And in Shakspeare (" Tempest," act iii. sc. 2):

STEPHANO: How now shall this be compassed? Canst thou bring me to the party?

CALIBAN: Yea, yea, my lord: I'll yield him thee asleep, where thou may'st knock a nail into his head.

And a correspondent quotes from Archbishop Ussher that, relating how he had been obliged to rebuke one of his clergy, he writes, "I sent for the party, and upon conference had with him, I put him in mind," &c. I once heard a venerable dignitary pointed out by a railway porter as "*an old party in a shovel.*" Curious is the idea raised in one's mind by hearing of "*a short party going over the bridge.*" Curious also that raised by an advertisement sent me; "Wanted, *a party* to teach a young man dancing *privately.* Apply, &c."

336. I have said that *party,* in its common untechnical use, signifies *man associated.* But we must remember that it has a technical use also. "I don't think," says a correspondent, "that party must mean '*man associated,*' but that it means one or more persons as regarded in relation to one or more others: and that by following out this, the passages in 'Tobit' and the 'Tempest' may be cleared, without giving any countenance to bagman's English. The *parties* (partes) in a lawsuit may be each a single person: and a clergyman who gives out a notice about 'these

[margin note:] Technical sense of "party"

parties being joined together,' although he
is wrong in departing from the Prayer-
book, does not seem to me incorrect in language."

"proceed." 337. The newspaper writers never allow us
to *go* anywhere, we always *proceed.* A man
going home, is set down as "an individual
proceeding to his *residence.*"

"partake." 338. We never *eat,* but always *partake,*
even though we happen to eat up the whole
of the thing mentioned. In court, counsel
asks a witness, "Did you have anything to
eat there?" "Yes." "What was it?" "A
bun." Now go to the report in the paper,
and you'll be sure to find that "witness confessed to having *partaken of* a bun," as if
some one else shared it with him.

"locality." 339. We never hear of a *place;* it is
always a *locality.* Nothing is ever *placed,*
but always *located.* "Most of the people of
the place" would be a terrible vulgarism to
these gentlemen; it must be "*the majority of
the residents in the locality.*"

"apart-
ments." 340. Then no one lives in *rooms,* but always
in "*apartments.*" "*Good lodgings*" would be
far too meagre; so we have "*eligible apartments.*"

"evince." 341. No man ever *shows* any feeling, but

always *"evinces"* it. This *"evince,"* by the way, is one of the most odious words in all this catalogue of vulgarities, for such they really are. Everybody *"evinces"* everything. No one *asks,* but *"evinces a desire."* No one is hurt, but *"evinces a sense of suffering."* No one thanks another, but *"evinces gratitude."* I remember, when the French band of the "Guides" were in this country, to have read in the *Illustrated News,* that as they *proceeded,* of course, along the streets of the *metropolis* (we never read of *London* in polite journals), they were *vehemently* (everybody does everything vehemently) cheered by the assembled *populace* (that is the genteel name for the people). And what do you suppose the Frenchmen did in return? Of course, something very different from what Englishmen would have done under similar circumstances. But did they toss up their caps, and cry, *Vive l'Angleterre?* The *Illustrated News* did not condescend to enter into such details; all it told us was, that they *"evinced a reciprocity"*!

342. Again, we never *begin* anything in the newspapers now, but always *commence.* I read lately in a Taunton paper, that a horse *"commenced kicking."* And the printers seem to

"commence."

think it quite wrong to violate this rule. Repeatedly, in drawing up handbills for charity sermons, I have written, as I always do, "Divine service will *begin* at so and so ;" but almost always it has been altered to "*commence ;*" and once I remember the bill being sent back after proof, with a "*query, commence ?*" written against the word. But even *commence* is not so bad as "*take the initiative,*" which is the newspaper phrase for the other more active meaning of the verb to *begin*.

"eventu-
ate."

343. Another horrible word, which is fast getting into our language through the provincial press, is to "*eventuate.*" If they want to say that a man spent his money till he was ruined, they tell us that *his unprecedented extravagance eventuated* in the total dispersion of his property.

"avoca-
tion."

344. "*Avocation*" is another monster patronised by these writers. Now *avocation*, which of itself is an innocent word enough, means the being called *away* from something. We might say, "He could not do it, having avocations elsewhere." But in our newspapers, *avocation* means a man's calling in life. If a shoemaker at his work is struck by lightning, we read, that "*while pursuing his avocation, the electric fluid penetrated the unhappy man's person.*"

345. "*Persuasion*" is another word very "persua-
commonly and very curiously used by them. sion."
We all know that *persuasion* means the fact of
being *persuaded*, by argument or by example.
But in the newspapers, it means a *sect* or *way
of belief*. And strangely enough, it is most
generally used of that very sect and way of
belief, whose characteristic is this, that they
refuse to be persuaded. We constantly read
of the "*Hebrew persuasion*," or the "*Jewish
persuasion*." I expect soon to see the term
widened still more, and a man of colour
described as "*an individual of the negro persuasion*."

346. Not only our rights of conscience, but "to sus-
even our sorrows are invaded by this terrible tain."
diluted English. In the papers, a man does
not now *lose his mother :* he "*sustains* (this I
saw in a country paper) *bereavement of his
maternal relative*." By the way, this verb *to
sustain* is doing just now a great deal of work
not its own. It means, you know, to endure, to
bear up under ; to *sustain* a bereavement, does
not properly mean merely to undergo or suffer
a loss, but to behave bravely under it. In
the newspapers, however, "*sustain*" comes in
for the happening to men of all the ills and
accidents possible. Men never break their

legs, but they always "*sustain a fracture*" of them ; a phrase which suggests to one the idea of the poor man with both hands holding up the broken limb to keep it straight.

"to expe-
rience." 347. Akin to *sustain* is the verb to *experience* now so constantly found in our newspapers. No one *feels*, but *experiences a sensation*. Now, in the best English, *experience* is a substantive, *not a verb at all*. But even if it is to be held (see above, paragraph 148), that the modern dialect has naturalized it, let us have it at least confined to its proper meaning, which is not simply to *feel*, but to have *personal knowledge of by trial*.*

"to accord." 348. Another such verb is to "*accord*," which is used for "*award*," or "adjudge." "*The prize was accorded*," we read, "*to so and so.*" If a lecturer is applauded at the end of his task, we are told that "*a complete ovation was accorded him.*"

" to entail." 349. *Entail* is another poor injured verb. Nothing ever *leads to* anything as a consequence, or brings it about, but it always *entails* it. This smells strong of the lawyer's clerk ; as does another word which we sometimes find in our newspapers, *in its entirety* instead of *all* or *the whole*.

* I read the other day in the *Times*, that the weather had experienced a change !

350. *Desirability* is a terrible word. I found it the other day, I think, in a leading article in the *Times.* And a correspondent sent me a quotation from the *Standard*, in which *displenishing* occurs.

"desira-
bility,"
"disple-
nishing."

351. *Reliable* is hardly legitimate. We do not *rely a man*, we *rely upon a man;* so that reliable does duty for *rely-upon-able.* "*Trustworthy*" conveys all the meaning required.

"reliable."

352. *Allude to* is used in a new sense by the journals, and not only by them, but also by the Government offices. If I have to complain to the Post-Office that a letter legibly directed to me at Canterbury has been missent to Caermarthen, I get a regular red-tape reply, beginning "The letter *alluded to* by you." Now I did not *allude to* the letter at all; I *mentioned* it as plainly as I could.

"allude."

353. I send a sentence to a paper to the following effect :—"When I came to the spot, I met a man running towards me with his hands held up." Next day I read, "When the very rev. gentleman arrived in close proximity to the scene of action, he encountered an individual proceeding at a rapid pace in the opposite direction, having both his hands elevated in an excited manner."

Examples of
the deterio-
ration.

354. This is fiction; but the following are

truth.   In a Somersetshire paper I saw that
a man had had his legs burned by sitting for
warmth, and falling asleep, on the top of a
lime-kiln.   The lime was called the "*seething
mass*" (to "*seethe*" means to *boil*,—and "*sad*,"
or "*sodden*," is its passive participle) ; and it
was said he would soon have been a *calcined
corpse,* which, I take it, would have been an
unheard-of chemical phenomenon.

355. In the same paper I read the following elegant sentence :—"Our prognostications
as regards the spirit of the young men here
to join the Stogursey rifle-corps proves correct."
The same paper, in commenting on the Hop-
ley case, speaks through a whole leading
article of *corporeal* punishment.   I may mention that, in this case, the accused person
figures throughout, as so often in provincial
papers, as a "*demon incarnate,*" and "*a fiend
in human shape.*"

356. In travelling up from Somersetshire
I find the directors of the Great Western
Railway thus posting up the want of a schoolmaster at their board: "£5 reward.   Whereas
the windows of the carriages, &c.   Whoever
will give *information as shall lead to conviction,*
shall receive the above reward ;" *as* being used
for *which :* "*the man as told me.*"

357. The South-Eastern directors seem to want the schoolmaster also. On the back of the tickets for the fast trains, we read the following precious piece of English grammar : —" This ticket is not transferable, only available for the station named thereon." This implying, of course, that using it for the station named on it, is *part of the process* of transferring it to some other person.

358. On a certain railway the following intelligible notice appears :—" Hereafter, when trains moving in an opposite direction are approaching each other on separate lines, conductors and engineers will be required to bring their respective trains to a dead halt before the point of meeting, and be very careful not to proceed till each train has passed the other."

359. In the *Morning Chronicle's* account of Lord Macaulay's funeral occurred the following sentence :—" When placed upon the ropes over the grave, and while being gradually lowered into the earth, the organ again pealed forth." Here, of course, on any possible grammatical understanding of the words, it was the *organ* which was placed over the grave, and was being lowered into the earth. Akin to this was the following notice, sent to

my house the other day by a jeweller :—" The brooches would have been sent before, but have been unwell."

A monster balloon.

360. After one of Mr. Glaisher's balloon ascents, we read that, " After partaking of a hearty breakfast, the balloon was brought into the town amidst the cheers and congratulations of the major part of the inhabitants." They may well have applauded a balloon which had performed so unheard-of a feat.

" so fully proved, than . ."

361. In a leading article of the *Times,* not long since, was this beautiful piece of slipshod English :—

" The atrocities of the middle passage, which called into action the Wilberforces and Clarksons of the last generation, were not so fully proved, and were certainly not more harrowing in their circumstances, than are the iniquities perpetrated upon the wretched Chinese."

362. Here you will observe we are by the form of the sentence committed to the combination of "were not so fully proved . . . than." This is a fault into which careless writers constantly fall : the joining together two clauses with a third, whose construction suits the latter of them, but not the former. " He was more popular, but not so much respected as his

father." Nothing can be easier than to avoid the fault. Transpose your third clause, letting it follow your first, and constructing it without reference to your second. "He was more popular than his father, but not so much respected." The mind of the hearer easily fills up the ellipsis after "respected," and the sentence sounds well. Thus the *Times'* writer might have said, "were not so fully proved as are the iniquities perpetrated upon the wretched Chinese, and were certainly not more harrowing in their circumstances."

363. There is another way, making the sentence correct indeed, but exceedingly clumsy. We *may* say, "He was more popular than, but not so much respected as, his father." But to my mind, this is almost worse than the incorrect sentence. It exhibits punctiliousness in all its stolidity, without any application of the sound, or effect, of the sentence.

364. And just let me, as I pass, notice one defence which has been deliberately set up for English of this kind. It has been said that one who sits in his study, writing, at leisure, may very well find time to look about him and weigh the structure of his sentences; but

Excuse of hasty writing.

s

that the contributors of articles to the daily press are obliged to write always in a hurry, and have no such opportunities of consideration.

365. Now this plea either fails in its object of excusing the practice complained of, or it proves too much. It fails, if it does not assign sufficient cause for the phenomenon: if, as I believe, it is not mere haste which causes a man to write such English as this, but deficiency in his power of putting thoughts into words: it proves too much, if it really does sufficiently excuse the writers; for if such writing is the inevitable result of the hasty publication of these critiques, why is not more time given for their production, and why are not more pains bestowed on them? For surely it is an evil, for a people to be daily accustomed to read English expressed thus obscurely and ungrammatically: it tends to confuse thought, and to deprive language of its proper force, and by this means to degrade us as a nation in the rank of thinkers and speakers.

Wonderful capacity of a windmill.

366. I am indebted for the following to a correspondent : — "To MILLERS. — To be let, a windmill, containing three pair of stones, a bakehouse, corn shop, and about

five acres of land, dwelling house, and garden."

366*a*. In the *Times*, a few days since, an advertisement thus ended : " If dead, his wife or children may apply."

Ghosts summoned by advertisement.

367. The following sentence, occurring in a hotel advertisement, may serve to illustrate a very common mistake : " Its night-watchman enables gentlemen to be called at any time, and, hourly patrolling the building, adds greatly to the comfort and security of all." Now we are sensible of an absurdity here. But what is the mistake ? It is not, you see, that some word, which to any ordinary reader has but one application, *may* be so combined as to bear other applications : but the incongruity is inevitable. A man who hourly patrols the building enables gentlemen to be called at any time : *i.e.*, by some arrangement which he makes, puts it in their power to be called, by somebody. Whereas the intention plainly was to notify that, owing to the fact of a night-watchman being employed, gentlemen can be called at any time by the night-watchman. The mistake is one easy to understand, though called by rather a hard name. It is the confounding of the abstract with the concrete. The fact of the night-

Powers of a night-watchman.

watchman being employed is in its nature abstract: is a consideration apart from persons and things which put it forth in action. This fact is independent of the particular man employed as night-watchman, and is the source of the advantages arising from it, whoever may happen to be so employed.

Inflated language in prayers.

368. I have received more than one letter from a gentleman who is much troubled by the inflated language of a book of prayers used in a school of small and ignorant boys. It would not become me to bring forward, as subjects for mirth, sentences and phrases whose meaning is so solemn : I can only deal with the complaint in a general way. And in doing so, I may say that there can hardly be a graver offence in the compilers of books of devotion, than this of using hard words and inflated sentences. If there is one essential requisite in a written prayer, it is, that it provide as much as possible for every word being understood and felt by those that are to use it. My correspondent tells me that the writer of whom he complains invariably uses *felicity* for happiness, *avocations* for employments, and the like. If I might presume to counsel the teachers of schools and heads of families, I would say, cast aside

every book of prayers which offends in this way. The simple and well-known collects of the Prayer-book, or even your own sense of the wants of your school or household, will furnish you with better, because more easy and real language of devotion than these high-flown manuals. And in default of either of these resources, I may venture to say that a school or a family rising from the reverent utterance of the Lord's prayer only, will have really *prayed* more, than one which has been wearied with ten minutes of a form such as that of which my correspondent complains.

369. Another criticism which I cannot help making, is on the practice of using, in general society, unmeaning and ridiculous familiar nicknames or terms of endearment. A more offensive habit cannot be imagined, or one which more effectually tends to the disparagement of those who indulge in it. I find myself, after the departure of the ladies from the dining-room, sitting next to an agreeable and sensible man. I get into interesting conversation with him. We seek a corner in the drawing-room afterwards, and continue it. His age and experience make him a treasure-house of information and practical wisdom. Yet, as talk trieth the man, infirmities begin

Nicknames and expressions of endearment.

to appear here and there, and my respect for my friend suffers diminution. By-and-by, a decided weak point is detected : and further on, it becomes evident that in the building up of his mental and personal fabric there is somewhere a loose stratum which will not hold under pressure. At last the servants begin to make those visits to the room, usually occurring about ten o'clock, which begin with gazing about, and result in a rush at some recognised object, with a summons from the coachman below. I am just doubting whether I have not about come to the end of my companion, when a shrill voice from the other side of the room calls out, "Sammy, love !" All is out. He has a wife who does not know better, and he has never taught her better. This is the secret. The skeleton in their cupboard is a child's rattle. A man may as well suck his thumb all his life, as talk, or allow to be talked to him, such drivelling nonsense. It must detract from manliness of character, and from proper self-respect : and is totally inconsistent with the good taste, and consideration, even in the least things, for the feelings of others, which are always present in persons of good breeding and Christian courtesy. Never let the world look through these chinks into the boudoir. Even thence, if there be real good sense present, all that is childish and ridiculous will be banished; but at all events keep it from the world. It is easy for husband and wife, it is easy for brothers and sisters, to talk to one another as none else could talk, without a word of this minced-up English. One soft tone, from lips on which dwells wisdom, is worth all the "loveys" and "deareys" which become the unmeaning expletives of the vulgar.

370. And as we have ventured to intrude into the boudoir, let us go one step further up, and peep into the nursery also. And here again I would say, never talk, never allow to be talked, to children, the contemptible nonsense which is so often the staple of nursery conversation. Never allow foolish and unmeaning nicknames to come into use in your family. We all feel, as we read of poor James I., with his "Steenie" for the Duke of Buckingham, and "Baby Charles" for his unfortunate son, that he cannot have been worthy to rule in England. We often find foolish names like these rooted in the practice of a family, and rendering grown-up men and women ridiculous in the eyes of strangers.

Talking nonsense to children.

And mind, in saying this, I have no wish to proscribe all abridgments, or familiar forms of names for our children, but only those which are unmeaning or absurd. I hold "Charley" to be perfectly legitimate : "Harry" is bound up with the glories of English history: Ned, and Dick, and Tom, and Jack, and Jem, and Bill, though none of them half so nice as the names which they have superseded, are too firmly fixed in English practice and English play, ever to be banished. Kate has almost become a name of itself; few maidens can carry the weight of Eleanor, whereas there never was a lass whom Nelly did not become. The same might be said of Milly and Amelia, and of many others. But the case of every one of such recognised nicknames differs widely from that, where some infantine lisping of a child's own name is adopted as the designation for life : or where a great rifleman with a bushy beard is called to hold his mamma's skein of wool by the astounding title of "Baby."

Sir J—M— and the tired nurse.

371. All perhaps do not know the story of the kind old gentleman and his carriage. He was riding at his ease one very hot day, when he saw a tired nursemaid toiling along the footpath, carrying a great heavy boy. His

heart softened : he stopped his carriage, and offered her a seat : adding, however, this : "Mind," said he, " the moment you begin to talk any nonsense to that boy, you leave my carriage." All went well for some minutes. The good woman was watchful, and bit her lips. But alas ! we are all caught tripping sometimes. After a few hundred yards, and a little jogging of the boy on her knee, burst forth, " Georgy porgy ! ride in coachy poachy !" It was fatal. The check-string was pulled, the steps let down, and the nurse and boy consigned to the dusty footpath as before.

372. This story is true. The person mainly concerned in it was a well-known philanthropic baronet of the last generation, and my informant was personally acquainted with him. A similar story, a correspondent reminds me, is told of Dr. Johnson.

373. As I am sending these sheets to the press, I receive a copy of the *Leeds Mercury* for Nov. 12, 1863, containing a leading article under the title of "English for the English," which touches on an abuse of our language unnoticed in these pages, but thoroughly deserving of reprobation. It is so appropriate to my present subject that I shall venture

Extract from the Leeds Mercury.

to cite a large portion of it almost as it stands.

374. "While the Dean," the writer says, "took so much trouble to expose one danger with which our mother tongue is threatened, he took no notice whatever of another peril which to us seems much more serious. He dealt only with the insubordinate little adverbs and pronouns of native growth, which sometimes intrude into forbidden places, and ignored altogether the formidable invasion of foreign nouns, adjectives, and verbs which promises ere long to transform the manly English language into a sort of mongrel international slang. A class of writers has sprung up who appear to think it their special business to 'enrich' the language by dragging into it, without any attempt at assimilation, contributions from all the tongues of the earth. The result is a wretched piece of patchwork, which may have charms in the eyes of some people, but which is certainly an abomination in the eyes of the genuine student of language."

375. "We need only glance into one of the periodical representatives of fashionable literature, or into a novel of the day, to see how

serious this assault upon the purity of the
English language has become. The chances
are more than equal that we shall fall in
with a writer who considers it a point of
honour to choose all his most emphatic words
from a French vocabulary, and who would
think it a lamentable falling off in his style,
did he write half a dozen sentences without
employing at least half that number of foreign
words. His heroes are always marked by an
air distingué; his vile men are sure to be
blasés; his lady friends never merely dance
or dress well, they dance or dress *à merveille;*
and he himself when lolling on the sofa under
the spirit of laziness does not simply enjoy
his rest, he luxuriates in the *dolce far niente*,
and wonders when he will manage to begin
his *magnum opus*. And so he carries us
through his story, running off into hackneyed
French, Italian, or Latin expressions, whenever he has anything to say which he thinks
should be graphically or emphatically said.
It really seems as if he thought the English
language too meagre, or too commonplace a
dress, in which to clothe his thoughts. The
tongue which gave a noble utterance to the
thoughts of Shakespere and Milton is altogether insufficient to express the more cos-

mopolitan ideas of Smith, or Tomkins, or Jenkins!"

376. "We have before us an article from the pen of a very clever writer, and, as it appears in a magazine which specially professes to represent the 'best society,' it may be taken as a good specimen of the style. It describes a dancing party, and we discover for the first time how much learning is necessary to describe a 'hop' properly. The reader is informed that all the people at the dance belong to the *beau monde,* as may be seen at a *coup d'œil;* the *demi-monde* is scrupulously excluded, and in fact everything about it bespeaks the *haut ton* of the whole affair. A lady who has been happy in her hair-dresser is said to be *coiffée à ravir.* Then there is the bold man to describe. Having acquired the *savoir faire,* he is never afraid of making a *faux pas,* but no matter what kind of conversation is started plunges at once *in medias res.* Following him is the fair *débutante,* who is already on the look-out for *un bon parti,* but whose *nez retroussé* is a decided obstacle to her success. She is of course accompanied by mamma *en grande toilette,* who, *entre nous,* looks rather *ridée* even in the gaslight. Then, lest the writer should seem

frivolous, he suddenly abandons the description of the dances, *vis-à-vis* and *dos-à-dos*, to tell us that Homer becomes tiresome when he sings of Βοῶπις πότνια Ἥρη twice in a page. The supper calls forth a corresponding amount of learning, and the writer concludes his article after having aired his Greek, his Latin, his French, and, in a subordinate way, his English."

377. "Of course, this style has admirers and imitators. It is showy and pretentious, and everything that is showy and pretentious has admirers. The admixture of foreign phrases with our plain English produces a kind of Brummagem sparkle which people whose appreciation is limited to the superficial imagine to be brilliance. Those who are deficient in taste and art education not unfrequently prefer a dashing picture by young Daub to a glorious cartoon by Raphael. The bright colouring of the one far more than counterbalances the lovely but unobtrusive grace of the other. In a similar way, young students are attracted by the false glitter of the French-paste school of composition, and instead of forming their sentences upon the beautiful models of the great English masters, they twist them into all sorts of unnatural

shapes for no other end than that they may introduce a few inappropriate French or Latin words, the use of which they have learned to think looks smart. Of course, the penny-a-liners are amongst the most enthusiastic followers of the masters of this style. They not only think it brilliant, but they know it to be profitable, inasmuch as it adds considerably to their ability to say a great deal about nothing. The public sees a great deal in the newspapers about 'recherché dinners' and 'sumptuous déjeûners' (sometimes eaten at night), and about the éclat with which a meeting attended by the 'élite of the county' invariably passes off; but they get but a trifling specimen of the masses of similar rubbish which daily fall upon the unhappy editors. The consequence of all this is that the public is habituated to a vicious kind of slang utterly unworthy to be called a language. Even the best educated people find it difficult to resist the contagion of fashion in such a thing as conversation, and if some kind of stand is not made against this invasion, pure English will soon only exist in the works of our dead authors."*

---

* A correspondent says, "In your next edition pray

378. "But it is not only on literary grounds that we think the bespanglement of our language with French and other foreign phrases is to be deprecated. Morality has something to say in the matter. It is a fact that things are said under the flimsy veil of foreign diction which could not very well be said in plain English. To talk in the presence of ladies about disreputable women by the plain English names which belong to them is not considered to display a very delicate mind, but anybody may talk about the *demi-monde* without fearing either a blush or a frown. Yet the idea conveyed is precisely the same in the one case as in the other; and inasmuch as words can only be indelicate when they convey an indelicate idea, we should think that the French words ought to be under the same disabilities as the English ones. In like manner, things sacred are often made strangely familiar by the intervention of a French dic-

dispose of those Gallicisms which are becoming too prevalent : 'The king *assisted at* the ceremony :' 'My brother has come to *pass* a few days with me :' instead of the English *was present* and *to spend.*" For the former of these there is, I believe, no excuse. But the latter usage, "passing time," is surely found in all periods of our literature ; and the good English substantive "*pastime*" is a voucher for it.

tionary. Persons whose reverence for the Deity is properly shown in their English conversation by a becoming unwillingness to make a light use of His holy Name, have no hesitation in exclaiming *Mon Dieu!* in frivolous conversation. The English name for the Father of evil is not considered to be a very reputable noun, but its French synonym is to be heard in 'the best society.' Far more telling illustrations than these could easily be found, but we have no inclination to seek them. Ideas which no decent person would ever think of expressing before a mixed company are certainly often spoken and written in French, and in our opinion they do not lose a particle of their coarseness by being dressed up in foreign clothes. We think, therefore, that the interests of morality as well as of pure taste concur in calling upon those who have influence with the public to set their faces against this vicious style."

379. I need not say that with every word of this I heartily concur. It is really quite refreshing to read in a newspaper, and a provincial one too, so able and honest an exposure of one of the worst faults of our daily and weekly press.

Use of expletives.

379*a*. I am tempted to add, in this second

edition, some remarks on the use, in speaking and writing, of terms which either seem to be, or really are, unneeded by the sense.

379*b*. To prohibit the use of expletives altogether, would perhaps seem hard. In conversation, they seem to help the timid, to give time to the unready, to keep up a pleasant semblance of familiarity, and, in a word, to grease the wheels of talk ; in writing, we often want them to redress the balance of a halting sentence, when any other way of doing so would mar the sense ; or to give weight to a term otherwise feeble, or to fill out a termination which, without them, would be insignificant in sound. For these reasons, the occasional use of expletives must be tolerated ; and that style of speaking or writing which should abandon them altogether would appear to us harsh and rugged.

379*c*. I said, the *occasional* use. Moderation ought to be observed : and where it is not, there is just ground for complaint. The man is properly found fault with who interlards his talk at every turn with "You see," and "You know." Both these terms have their use, and if that use be disregarded in an indiscriminate profusion of them, they will become vapid and meaningless. They serve,

T

when used as quasi-expletives, just to keep the hearer up to the mark of the knowledge you are imparting to him, and should be used only as applying to facts or ideas of which he is, or should be, already in possession.

"well," "why."

379*d*. There are other expletives which serve merely to indicate the sequence of the course of talk, or the frame of mind in which it is continued. A simple question is asked; and your friend's answer begins with " *Well.*" Little as the word means, it just does this service : it puts the respondent *en rapport* with the questioner : he intends by it to say that he does not absolutely repudiate the inquiry : that, so far, is *well*, and that we have common ground up to this point. Or the first word of the answer is " *Why,*—" a particle, of which the meaning is not quite so easy to assign ; but I suppose it gives a kind of dubitative aspect to what follows : introduces a deliberative and not quite certain reply ; or perhaps slightly rallies the querist on some obvious element in the reply which his question shows him to have overlooked. " What would you do first, if you were to fall down ?" " Why get up again, of course." So that the use of such prefatory particles is, I conceive, by no means to be proscribed. It

should however in the main be confined to
oral communication or dramatic dialogue, and
not be admitted in the style of a writer.

379*e*. Yet even in written composition "at all."
there are certain expressions more or less
nearly approaching to expletives, the use of
which cannot well be prohibited. I am
challenged by one of my correspondents, who
gives a list of sentences in which I have used
the expression "*at all*," to say what difference
in the meaning of any of them there would
be if the words were struck out. My answer
must be, in accordance with the foregoing
remarks, that the difference in meaning would
perhaps not be great, but it would be quite
enough to justify the use of the words, as any
intelligent reader may at once perceive.
" Thou hast not delivered thy people *at all*"
(Exod. v. 23), is surely very distinct, at all
events in the feeling of utter desolation expressed, from " Thou hast not delivered thy
people." " If thou do *at all* forget the Lord"
(Deut. viii. 19), makes the hypothesis much
more complete than it would be without the
qualifying words. Or, to take another notable
example, where the difference would seem to
be less than in the others, " God is light, and
in Him is no darkness *at all*" (1 John i. 5),

who does not see that by the words *"at all"*
every possibility of even the least shade of
darkness existing in Him is altogether excluded? So that, when my correspondent
designates these words as a feeble expletive,
which adds nothing to the meaning of the
sentence to which it is attached, I cannot
agree with his opinion, nor do I think that
the majority of my readers will.

379*f.* If the origin of the phrase is to be
sought for, I know not any other than may
be found in the requirements of speech itself.
What the Apostle, in the original Greek of 1
John i. 5, expressed by the strong double
negation, σκοτία ἐν αὐτῷ οὐκ ἔστιν οὐδεμία,
we could not in English render by "there is
not in Him no darkness," because in our
language the doubling of a negation destroys
instead of strengthening it : we had recourse
to another way of expressing total exclusion,
"there is in Him no darkness *at all ;*" "*at
all,*" *i. e.*, taking the assertion even up to the
measure of all,—"*altogether,*"—providing for,
and taking into consideration, every sup-
posable exception, every qualifying circumstance. The preposition "*at,*" in this phrase,
has the same sense as in "*at least,*" "*at best,*"
and the like.

379*g.* "*And the like.*" This is also desig- "and the like." nated by my correspondent as a feeble expletive, and indeed as an "*Irishism.*" No doubt it may be so used as to *become* an expletive; but I am not conscious of having so used it: at least, in every one of the sentences which he quotes, it does full service, as shortly comprehending other examples of the same kind as those already cited.

379*h.* Let me say a word on expletives of Unmeaning exclamations. another kind: exclamations of surprise, or of any other feeling, which taken by themselves carry no meaning. It is perhaps impossible to avoid them altogether: speech will break out when emotion is excited: and "*You don't say so,*" or "*Indeed!*", or "*Dear me!*" is sometimes heard even from persons best able to give an account of what they say. Yet it may not be amiss to remember, that idle words are seldom quite harmless; and to impress on ourselves, that the fewer we use of such expletives the better. This was strikingly brought before me during intercourse with Italians last winter in Rome. I had observed that my Italian friends often in their talk uttered some sounds very like our "dear, dear!" and at first I thought that my ear must have deceived me. But I soon found that it was so : and that sometimes the exclamation even took the form of *" dear me !"* The explanation of course is obvious. The Italians were exclaming *" Dio, Dio !"* and the fuller form was *" Dio mio !"* And the reflection arising from it was as obvious : *viz.*, that it thus seems probable that our unmeaning words, *" dear, dear !"* and *" dear me !"* are, in fact, nothing but a form of taking the sacred Name in vain, borrowed from the use of a people with whom we were once in much closer intercourse than we now are. Thus it would seem that the *idle* word is not quite free from blame.

Concluding advice.

380. But it is time that this little volume drew to an end. And if I must conclude it with some advice to my readers, it shall be that which may be inferred from these examples, and from the way in which I have been dealing with them. Be simple, be unaffected, be honest in your speaking and writing. Never use a long word where a short one will do. Call a spade a spade, not *a well-known oblong instrument of manual industry ;* let home be *home,* not a *residence ;* a place a *place,* not a *locality ;* and so of the rest. Where a short word will do, you always lose by using a long one. You lose in clearness ;

you lose in honest expression of your meaning; and, in the estimation of all men who are qualified to judge, you lose in reputation for ability. The only true way to shine, even in this false world, is to be modest and unassuming. Falsehood may be a very thick crust, but in the course of time, truth will find a place to break through. Elegance of language may not be in the power of all of us; but simplicity and straightforwardness are. Write much as you would speak; speak as you think. If with your inferiors, speak no coarser than usual; if with your superiors, no finer. Be what you say; and, within the rules of prudence, say what you are.

381. Avoid all oddity of expression. No one ever was a gainer by singularity in words, or in pronunciation. The truly wise man will so speak, that no one may observe how he speaks. A man may show great knowledge of chemistry by carrying about bladders of strange gases to breathe; but he will enjoy better health, and find more time for business, who lives on the common air. When I hear a person use a queer expression, or pronounce a name in reading differently from his neighbours, the habit always goes down, in my estimate of him, with a *minus sign*

before it; stands on the side of deficit, not of credit.

382. Avoid likewise all *slang* words. There is no greater nuisance in society than a talker of slang. It is only fit (when innocent, which it seldom is) for raw schoolboys, and one-term freshmen, to astonish their sisters with. Talk as sensible men talk: use the easiest words in their commonest meaning. Let the sense conveyed, not the vehicle in which it is conveyed, be your object of attention.

383. Once more, avoid in conversation all singularity of accuracy. One of the bores of society is the talker who is always setting you right; who, when you report from the paper that 10,000 men fell in some battle, tells you it was 9,970; who, when you describe your walk as two miles out and back, assures you it wanted half a furlong of it. Truth does not consist in minute accuracy of detail, but in conveying a right impression; and there are vague ways of speaking, that are truer than strict fact would be. When the Psalmist said, "Rivers of waters run down mine eyes, because men keep not thy law," he did not state the fact, but he stated a truth deeper than fact, and truer.

384. Talk to please, not yourself, but your

neighbour to his edification. What a real pleasure it is to sit by a cheerful, unassuming, sensible talker ; one who gives you an even share in the conversation and in his attention ; one who leaves on your memory his facts and his opinions, not himself who uttered them, not the words in which they were uttered.

385. All are not gentlemen by birth ; but all may be gentlemen in openness, in modesty of language, in attracting no man's attention by singularities, and giving no man offence by forwardness ; for it is this, in matter of speech and style, which is the sure mark of good taste and good breeding.

386. These stray notes on spelling and speaking have been written more as contributions to discussion, than as attempts to decide in doubtful cases. The decision of matters such as those which I have treated is not made by any one man or set of men ; cannot be brought about by strong writing, or vehement assertion : but depends on influences wider than any one man's view, and taking longer to operate than the life of any one generation. It depends on the direction and deviations of the currents of a nation's thoughts, and the influence exercised on

Conclusion.

words by events beyond man's control. Grammarians and rhetoricians may set bounds to language : but usage will break over in spite of them. And I have ventured to think that he may do some service who, instead of standing and protesting where this has been the case, observes, and points out to others, the existing phenomena, and the probable account to be given of them.

NOTES.

NOTE A.

Mr. Serjeant Manning has published a very interesting and learned pamphlet on "the Character and Origin of the Possessive Augment in English and its Cognate Dialects." Without pronouncing any opinion as to the theory which the learned Serjeant adopts, I may say that the reader will find in his pamphlet a very full and instructive discussion of all points relating to the question, coupled with an extraordinary amount of information and erudition. He describes himself as "*annum agens octogesimum tertium ;*" a circumstance which does not render the book less remarkable.

NOTE B.

These paragraphs have provoked a somewhat vehement rejoinder in a late number of a nonconformist newspaper, in which they are characterised as "a sufficiently ill-intentioned, if not very powerful, assault" on that journal. Two remarks may be pertinent in reply. The first, that no assault on any paper, as such, was ever contemplated by me, but as strong a protest as I could make against the most objectionable principle laid down in the critique, and an endeavour, by exposure of the blunder, to show how much the opinion was worth. The blunder is now rather amusingly defended thus : "We accidentally substituted for the less known

Epænetus what is to the classical scholar the more familiar and analogously formed name Sophænetus." Now as regards the *classical scholar*,—Epænetus, the writer on cookery, is about as often mentioned in Athenæus, as Sophænetus in Xenophon : and the matter in question being *St. Paul's lists of salutations*, I do not see why the critic should have gone to Xenophon for his example, unless he had believed that the name occurred in St. Paul also.

The second remark shall be an extract from a letter written by one of the first nonconformist biblical scholars of the day :—" I felt rather vexed, that so respectable a newspaper should have inserted the inexcusably stupid and grossly ignorant remarks of one of its correspondents, in reference to your articles on the Queen's English."

NOTE C.

There is an especial reason for stating that this sentence is printed *verbatim* as delivered in St. George's Hall, at Canterbury.

NOTE D.

I have been favoured with some notices from a distinguished correspondent, which have caused me to alter what was in the first edition the tone of these paragraphs as regarded the phrases in question. There seems every reason to believe that *kind* and *sort* have been regarded by our best writers as nouns of number, and as such joined with the pronoun in the plural. Thus we have in Shakespeare, "King Lear," Act II., Scene 2 :

"These kind of knaves I know."

"Twelfth Night," Act I., Scene 5 :

> "That crow so at these kind of fools."

"Othello," Act III., Scene 3 :

> "There are a kind of men so loose in soul."

In Pope :

"The next objection is, that these sort of authors are poor."

Examples are also stated to occur in Lord Bacon, Swift, and Addison.

NOTE E.

It has been suggested that the "*of*" in "*the city of Canterbury,*" may be *territorial* : that as it is rendered in Latin by "*de,*" this "*de*" may be the same that we find in "*Henricus de Estria.*" But I cannot quite agree with this view : because though it might seem to be justified in the case of a town, it clearly would not be in that of a book, or in any other in which the territorial connexion is out of the question.

NOTE F.

I venture to reprint here, as of great interest, Mr. Ellis's letter to the *Reader*, of May 7, 1864 :

"'IT'S ME.

"*To the Editor of* THE READER.

"Colney Hatch Park, 30 April, 1864.

"SIR,—In reference to your remarks on *it's me* in your notice of Dean Alford's 'Plea for the Queen's English,' I consider that the phrase *it is I* is a modernism, or rather a grammaticism—that is, it was never in popular use, but was introduced solely on some grammatical hypothesis as to having the same case before and after the verb *is*. It does not appear to have been consonant with the feelings of Teutonic tribes to use the nominative of the personal pronouns as a predicate. To them—and therefore to English people—*it is I* is just as strange as *est ego*, ἐστὶ ἐγώ, would be to Latin or Greek. These last languages require *ego sum*, ἐγώ εἰμι (Matt. xiv. 27; Mark vi. 50; John vi. 20). The predicate was here simply omitted. In Gothic we have precisely the same construction, *ik im* (John vi. 20). The English Wycliffite translations both give *I am*. But the Anglo-Saxon version, like the modern German, is not content with leaving the predicate unexpressed, and we find *ic hit eom;* High German, *ich bin es;* literally, *I am it;* namely, *that which you see*. The Heliand paraphrase is very explicit (Schmeller's ed., p. 90, line 2), '*Ik bium that barn Godes*' ('I am the Son of God'). The Welsh and Gaelic try to be emphatic, the first saying *myfi ydyw* (q. d. myself am), and the second, *is mise a ta ann* (q. d. it's myself that's living). But of course we do not look to these languages as a guide to English. The Danish is very peculiar and important on account of its intimate relation with English. As in English, the dative and accusative cases of the personal pronouns now coincide in Danish, *Jeg, mig* (I, me); *Du, dig* (thou, thee); *Han, ham* (he, him). We find the following rule laid down in Tobiesen's *Dänische Sprachlehre* (Sternhagen's ed., 1828, p. 215):—'After the impersonal verbs, *det er* and *det bliver* (it is), the personal pronouns *jeg, du, han* are not used in the nominative, but in the dative, as *der er mig der har gjort det* (it's me that did it); *det er dig, som har været mester derfor* (it's thee who was its master); *det bliver ham, som vi ville tale med* (it's him that we wish to speak with); [where also the construction of the relative and preposition is English]; and similarly in the plural: *det er os, jer, dem* (it's us, you, them).' This is perfectly explicit, and shows the same construction as the English; but, in the Testament, the wish to be uncolloquial has apparently forced the translator to depart from the usual custom when the words are given to Jesus, but he returns to it when they are echoed by Peter (Matt. xiv. 27, 28). '*Jesus—sagde :—det er jeg, —men Peder—sagde : Herre, dersom det er dig, ba byd mig,*' &c. ('Jesus said, It is I ; but Peter said, Lord, if it is *thee,* bid me,' &c.) The conclusion seems to be that *it's me* is good English, and *it's I* is a mistaken purism. We have now, I think, come to regard the objective form of the personal pronoun as a *predicative* form, and this will justify *that's him,* although the Danes still say '*denne er han*' ('that's he'). We are therefore in the same condition as the French with their '*c'est moi,*' though we have not quite reached their '*lui n'osait pas*' ('*him* didn't dare').

"Alexander J. Ellis."

It will be curious if, after all, it should be proved that our much-abused colloquial phrase is the really good English, and its rival "a mistaken purism."

ADDITIONAL NOTE.

A friend has directed my attention to the fact that in "The New Whig Guide," printed in 1824, the word "*talented*" is noticed as an Irish expression, equivalent to the English "*clever.*"

THE END.